DIANA RIGG

THE BIOGRAPHY

Also by Kathleen Tracy

• • • •

Ellen: The Real Story of Ellen DeGeneres

Home-Brewed: The Drew Carey Story

Jerry Seinfeld, the Entire Domain

Dixie Chicks

The Boy Who Would Be King: An Intimate Portrait of Elvis Presley by His Cousin (with Earl Greenwood)

DIANA RIGG
THE BIOGRAPHY

• • • •

KATHLEEN TRACY

BenBella Books
Dallas, Texas

First BenBella Books Edition May 2004

BenBella Books
6440 N. Central Expressway, Suite 508
Dallas, TX 75206

Send feedback to feedback@benbellabooks.com
www.benbellabooks.com

Printed in the United States of America
10 9 8 7 6 5 4 3 2 1

Tracy, Kathleen.
    Diana Rigg : the biography / by Kathleen Tracy.
        p. cm.
    ISBN 1-932100-27-X
    1. Rigg, Diana. 2. Actors—Great Britain—Biography. I. Title.

PN2598.R47T73 2004
791.43′028′092--dc22

                        2003025528

Cover design by Andy Carpenter
Interior designed and composed by Melody Cadungog

Distributed by Independent Publishers Group
To order call (800) 888-4741
www.ipgbook.com

Introduction

DIANA Rigg is a study in glorious contradictions. She is one of the English-speaking world's greatest dramatic actors who is best known for a short-lived stint in a television comedy. After decades of working nonstop she happily put her career on hold for over ten years to raise her daughter. She was the first kick-your-ass, empowered woman on television but refuses to consider herself a feminist; she is a Dame who considers herself a dame; she is a desired iconic sex symbol who intimidates men with her keen intelligence; she is a middle-class Yorkshire girl who became a theater legend.

Throughout her career and life, Dame Diana Rigg has been a relentless groundbreaker, not because of any personal agenda but rather because it was simply her nature to challenge herself and any conventions that happened to be in the way. At the same time, she fiercely balanced her life with her art. Because Rigg has spent most of her career on the British stage and has stubbornly refused to relocate to Hollywood to pursue a feature-film career, there are many who only know her from *The Avengers* or as the host of the PBS anthology *Mystery!*. But in between those two programs Rigg amassed a wealth of professional achievements and balanced that with a private life as dramatically full and wittily captivating as some of her greatest roles, sometimes at the expense of her career.

"Deep down I have an irreverent spirit," explains Rigg. "People who take themselves deeply seriously are really good at tragedy, and I don't take myself that seriously. I could have gone on and done greater things but I didn't. It's as simple as that."

Actually, few things in Dame Diana's life were ever that simple.

CHAPTER ONE

• • • •

To the British in the early twentieth century India was nothing short of the jewel in their crown, the most glorious and important colony of the empire.

When the British Crown took over direct control from the East India Company in 1857 it inherited over 750,000 square miles of territory. For whatever ills India suffered at the hands of colonialism, the enduring legacy of Britain was the railway system it built to connect the wide-ranging cities dotting the vast countryside. In its heyday the Indian rail network was the largest on Earth. Besides being a practical way to transport goods, the trains were also widely used by the British colonials.

Each railway system, such as the East India Railway Company or the Bengal Railway Company, was independently owned and operated. While the railways were a visual symbol of the British Raj, or rule, they were also vehicles of national unity. The trains helped distribute food in times of famine and opened up trade. More importantly, they were the greatest private employers in India, hiring both men and women of all castes. The rail companies also built hospitals and schools for employees and offered company housing. Working for the railway was considered the best job in government service. For the British railway managers life in India was positively royal. The East India Railway town in the Jamalpur district had swimming pools, tennis courts and also a Masonic Lodge; even the managers lived in palatial company houses.

By the early twentieth century the Indian rail system was thriving, but new tracks were continually being built and the need for British engineers remained high. In 1925 a tall, slender young man from Doncaster, Yorkshire, named Louis Rigg came to answer a job listing in the *Times* newspaper. Previously, Louis—who was called James by his friends and family—had won a scholarship to become an engineering apprentice and was anxious to find a job. Just twenty-two and coming from a lower middle-class family, Louis was willing to travel halfway around the world for a chance to work in exotic India for a good wage and steady employment.

Louis spent five years in India before returning to England. While relaxing at a local tennis club, Louis met a young woman named Beryl Helliwell; they fell in love and when it came time for Louis to return to India, Beryl accompanied him. They were married in Bombay Cathedral in 1932 and moved into a bungalow at Bikaner, located in the state of Rajasthan, situated on India's western border. Two years later Beryl gave birth to a son they named Hugh, who was born in a military hospital. Four years later she got pregnant again, but this time she traveled to Britain for the birth of their second baby, Diana. Diana Rigg would later comment that her mother had such a terrible experience at the military hospital during Hugh's birth that she insisted on returning to England to deliver her second child. Plus, England must have seemed a very appealing way to avoid the brutal Indian summer heat. On July 20, 1938 Diana Rigg was born in the South Yorkshire town of Doncaster. Just two months later Beryl returned to India to rejoin her husband and young son.

The colonial India of Diana's childhood provided for an exotic upbringing. Both Bikaner and Jodhpur, where her family moved in 1943, are filled with magnificent palaces and forts, remnants of earlier times when other states posed the threat of invasion. They are perched at the edge of the Thar Desert, also known as the Great Indian Desert, and during the summer temperatures regularly reach 115 degrees. Anyone with the means would head to the hills during the sweltering summers. Despite the heat, the landscape held a harsh beauty. There are no oases or artesian wells in the Great Indian Desert, so there are no native cacti decorating the landscape, which alternates between sand, scrubby hills and gravelly plains. But there is abundant reptilian wildlife, with dozens of thriving lizard and snake species, which the Riggs and others living in the region learned to avoid.

Tall and slender, Diana was a tomboy as a child and says, "For Hugh and I India was a wonderful adventure but with some frights for my mother. She shrieked if we went out without our *topis*, and there were snakes everywhere, particularly in the bathrooms. The gardener showed us a snake nest once and we saw the babies in their eggs."

Diana remembers living in a big house. "We had gardeners and what were called servants in those days. It was very British Raj. In terms of the Raj hierarchy, though, my father wasn't high up the ladder. But they used to go to astonishing banquets at the palace. I've still got the menu cards. My mother would describe some exquisite confection on her plate, made from spun sugar. I remember how she said, 'I simply had to tap it with my spoon for it to shatter, it was so delicate.'"

Diana and her brother lived near the railways; they grew up in the shadow of the majestic train stations where beggars and British aristocracy alike waited to board. Of course, the cabs used by the sahibs and memsahibs (as wealthy Europeans were called) were starkly different from those used by the poor. Rigg would later recall, "We went to the hills in the hot season much as the Royal Family travels to Balmoral—in our own carriage," referring to the plush private rail cars they rode in. Now that their engineer father had risen through the ranks to railway superintendent, they were afforded the comforts and advantages that came with the position. "I remember the smell of oil and metal. This was Dad's kingdom. He loved it so much."

Summers were spent in Nainital, an area in the Himalayan foothills also called the Lake District. "Mother allowed us to run wild," Diana told the *London Daily Telegraph* in a 2002 interview. "We disappeared every day, though we came back for lunch. I remember sucking the toffee my mother used to make, reading Jim Corbett's *Maneaters of Kumaon* with the rain thundering on the roof. And I remember my father reading Kipling to me." Diana recalls her father reading to her Kipling's *Just So Stories* and Tolkien's *The Hobbit*. "India gave me a glorious start to life. It gave me an independence of spirit. Our parents lived very social lives and took us on lovely family outings."

The rest of the year was spent in Bikaner. Their house was a bungalow, which is actually derived from the Hindi word *bangle*, roughly translated as "house in the Bengali style": a one-story home with a low, pitched roof. We've come to think of bungalows as being small and cozy, but the family home in India was spacious and came complete with a fireplace. Although the temperatures soared in summer, the winter evenings were cool. Outside, there was a large front lawn, where Hugh could play cricket with local boys or he and Diana could spend the afternoon riding ponies.

Like many other British families in India, the Riggs had several servants and Diana was cared for by a nanny, called an ayah, who taught her Hindi. "The ayah would say, *'aap bahut hi badmash ladki hain'*—you're a very bad girl—and my mother told me I talked like an Indian," Diana recalled to Trevor Fishlock during a trip back to India in 2002. "My mother tried to keep things English and gave us the nearest thing to English food, a lot of it from tins and disgusting; although her sardine kedgeree was delicious." Remembering the nanny and the servants, Rigg recalls wistfully, "They all spoiled me."

Although Louis had been born without means, his job at the railway had brought him financial success and prestige.

As a result, Louis and Beryl found themselves moving in ever higher social circles among the British in India. "It was a social leap for both of them," Diana told Fishlock. "Mother had to learn quickly to run a house with servants and adjust to the social conventions of the Raj, which were strict and without mercy or pity. But they lived happy lives of privilege. Dad was an excellent shot and a brilliant golfer, tennis and squash player. These qualities made him welcome. And he was also a witty, handsome man with great social ease." Rigg also recalls that her dad liked to fish, a hobby she would take up years later as an adult, noting she is "quite good at seeking out the gentleman's fish, the one that isn't actually sitting up and begging to be caught."

Louis not only managed to fit in with the expatriate aristocrats, but he was also respected by the Indians who worked with him because he was seen as someone who did not lord his position over them. One of Hugh Rigg's most vivid memories of his dad was seeing him come home after work, plop down in his favorite chair and relax with a whisky and soda brought to him by one of the servants.

Despite her fond memories of her parents, Rigg admitted in a *Oui* interview that she often felt separate from them. "My parents were rather Edwardian. I didn't see a great deal of them. Ayah, my Indian nanny, was around. I saw more of my mother during the hot season when we went out into the hills, but I spent a lot of time on my own reading." Her father was equally elusive, although he did take the time to teach her how to fry fish.

But Diana's feelings of isolation were about to be dramatically compounded. In 1945, when Diana was eight, Louis and Beryl sent her back to England to attend school. Not only had World War II ended, but the days of the British Raj were quickly drawing to a close. In a little over two years, on August 15, 1947, India would gain independence and the colonial way of life would be forever extinguished.

Even though she was returning to her native land, Diana felt like a refugee and had to adjust to jarring culture shock. Compared to the vibrant pageantry that marked British India, where she ran free and had the attention of the servants and her nanny, being sent off to a British boarding school was akin to a jail sentence. She was miserably unhappy. "My parents didn't mean to be cruel," she said in a *Sunday Times* interview. "It was a matter of convenience for my parents; they thought they were doing the right thing. Your parents are three weeks away by boat and you can't telephone them. The school didn't mean to be cruel but it was. I felt like a fish out of water. I knew nobody. I started from scratch." Moreover, the weather was dank and cold; she developed an earache and caught lice. "With an experience like that your life changes," Rigg added. "There is a sense of rejection and you have to take care of yourself. You are never reliant on your parents again."

To comfort herself, she began tapping into her imagination. "You have an inner life very quickly that sustains you," she explained in a *TV Times* interview. "And children are very adaptable. You know, I wasn't actively unhappy but I became very self-sufficient. I would remember images of glamour from the only film I'd seen—*The Red Shoes*—and use them to imagine myself as a different person. I used my imagination to transport me from the distress of my environment." Diana would often seek out solitude by climbing to the top of a tree in the school grounds, "high, high up." She explained, "I sensed a communion up there." During holidays, she would stay with her grandmother in Doncaster "who was quite cross at having two children to look after," all the while feeling abandoned by her parents. "My parents made mistakes which people simply wouldn't do now," she said.

But as she adjusted, Rigg began to make friends and soon found herself enjoying her new surroundings at Great Missenden School in Buckhinghamshire. She employed her imagination to captivate the others and became known as a good storyteller, using her adventures in India as the basis for many of her tales. It was then that her resistance to authority began to express itself, and Diana told *Cosmopolitan* in 1976 that she found kindred spirits among the other girls. "The first school I went to was absolutely fascinating. I'm still friendly with a lot of the girls who were there. That school, I suspect, sowed the seeds of what we all were to become later on. It was a bit like Mary McCarthy's *The Group*. We were incredibly rebellious. But it's understandable because it was a boarding school and most of our parents were abroad. We hadn't seen them for stretches of two or three years, so we became very independent, rather like the savage boy-band in *Lord of the Flies*. We didn't exactly kill each other but we had that capacity, we had that freedom." Which is what made it such a jolt when Diana's parents returned to England from India for good.

"It was tough when my parents came back from abroad and I was pulled into a family unit which, during two very formative years of my life, I had done without," Rigg admits. "I found that extremely difficult." The family problems were compounded by Louis's inability to find a job and the distance Diana felt from her mother. Rigg immersed herself in literature as a means to escape. "I listened to the wonderful plays on the wireless and my imagination was lit by poetry and words. It was the start of a journey that involved feeding my mind."

Diana lost more emotional equilibrium a year later when she was moved to a school closer to Leeds, where her family settled after Louis was hired as works manager of an engineering firm. She explains, "I changed schools and found myself in this very rigid, very Quaker establishment. So I was quite a loner."

Fulneck Girls' School, named after a German town, is located in the former mill town of Pudsey, Yorkshire, where a group of Moravian religious refugees from Germany settled in 1742. The Moravian Church, officially named Unity of the Brethren, is an ancient protestant Episcopal church founded in 1457 in Moravia by the followers of religious reformer John Hus. Hus was a priest who preached that the Bible should be the final authority in Christianity, taking precedence over any man or clergy, including the pope. Predictably, this didn't sit well at the Vatican, so Hus was excommunicated and condemned as a heretic at the Council of Constance for his uncompromising belief. He refused to recant and was burned at the stake on July 6, 1415, on his forty-sixth birthday. His followers were also persecuted. Literally feeling the heat, they migrated west and through their missionaries set up various settlements in Europe, including the one in Yorkshire.

Considering the Moravian background, it's not surprising that the students attending Fulneck Girls' School were not exactly bathed in personal freedom. In a word, Rigg found the school loathsome. "It was very rigid, very strict, very cruel. I was quite unhappy," she recalled on several occasions. "We wore a school uniform, thick brown stockings in winter, gymslips, blouses and ties. Classes were incredibly boring. I took to dreaming."

Even so, Rigg wouldn't describe herself as being withdrawn. "No, I don't think so," she said in a *TV Times* interview. "I had the ability to withdraw and I still have it. But above all I always had a strong sense of personal identity."

Rigg told *Cosmopolitan* that students were intellectually stifled. "You were not allowed to question anything at all. Ugliness, physical ugliness, was what seemed most acceptable. We wore hideous uniforms and weren't allowed to wear our hair in any attractive fashion. It was either in plaits or stuffed into your collar. You were made to kneel on the floor and your gymslip had to be three inches above your knees when you're kneeling. Every aspect of life there was so *measurable*. They took to punishing me. I was always working off punishments for not doing what I was supposed to. I was tall and redheaded. Tall redheads always get caught." Why Rigg's parents subjected their daughter to such an environment has never been publicly addressed. But if they were trying to squelch a streak of independence they didn't understand and that was alien to their sensibilities, the preemptive strike was doomed to fail.

Despite all the unhappiness she experienced at Fulneck, or perhaps precisely because of it, Diana discovered a simmering passion and talent, thanks in part to her elocution teacher Sylvia Greenwood, who was impressed with Rigg's voice and budding dramatic flair. "It's always down to a teacher, isn't it?" she observed. "She had white hair, even at forty, wonderful skin, big blue eyes. She was plump and passionate about Shakespeare and she was determined I was going to be an actress." Rigg told *FInterview* magazine in 1973 that the teacher undeniably changed her life. "I was a big, lumpy girl. Sylvia Greenwood realized I loved literature, and words, and saw that I could speak and—well, act! Not just encouraged me, she cheered me on, brought me out. I began to live. I used to go home every night and lock myself in my bedroom and spout verse. So I began to think, '*This is what I want. This is being alive.*' And I soon concluded that *this* could only be made available by going on the stage."

Rigg had felt the inkling before when she had once found a red chiffon ball gown in her mother's closet and, putting it on, discovered she could for that moment be someone else. "That was it," Diana told the *Sunday Times*, recalling the feeling she had seeing herself in the dress. "Cocteau called love of theater 'the red and gold disease'. Mine was just red. I hadn't seen a stage, I'd just looked and seen myself transformed. It wasn't a vision about acting but about the process of becoming something else." She would also tell Henry Gris that the appeal of acting had nothing to do with the profession's more glamorous perks. "One thing that I never did was dream. I was always very practical. I grew interested in the theater when I was small but not because it offered me an entrance to a world of fantasy, but because it gave me a chance to assert myself. And I loved its freedom."

Diana worked diligently on her poetry recital and was encouraged and supported by her grandfather who "would have me stand and say *The Highwayman*," she said. She loved the lyric poets, T.S. Eliot and Shakespeare—"always Shakespeare." She played Titania the fairy queen in a Fulneck production of *A Midsummer Night's Dream*, looking, she says, "lumpish in my brown stockings." While her parents played bridge, she would be snuggled near the radio listening raptly to *Saturday Night Theatre*. And after Louis and Beryl took her to see a production of *Henry VIII* when she was twelve, Rigg knew for certain she would pursue acting as a career. She was so inspired by the play, she begged her parents to take her to see it a second time. Rigg was further seduced by her muse after starring as Goldilocks in another school production when she was thirteen.

But sometimes Diana felt undermined by her family, which frowned on vanity. The lessons were subtle but clear. When she was a child, bread with jam and butter was never allowed before a slice of plain bread had first been consumed. "My family—and this is very Yorkshire—sat on you," she explained to *Cosmopolitan*. "If my grandmother caught me looking in the mirror, she'd say, 'Vanity, vanity,' or, 'What are you looking at, silly little face?'—a real put down. I remember at Sunday supper she always served pickled beetroot and I put a tiny bit of beetroot on my fork and rubbed it over my lips and tried to sneak a look to see what I looked like with lipstick. I was caught and slapped down mightily.

"I used to look at myself in the mirror when I was thirteen or fourteen and know what I saw was not me. It was curious seeing the chrysalis, finding it insufficient and yet knowing that something inside there was going to pop out, was going to be better. Had to be. Thank God." Rigg, though, didn't lack for love. "My parents loved me and they were wonderful people, but it was generational," she said. "I was The Child even when I was thirty-five. We were a close family. But there are vast areas of me because I don't think I belong anywhere. I think that is what led me to the theater."

That, and Sylvia Greenwood. "She persuaded my parents, who were incredibly doubtful about the whole thing," Rigg told the *Daily Telegraph*. Diana graduated from Fulneck when she was seventeen, and emboldened by her performance in *Goldilocks*, she auditioned for the Royal Academy of Dramatic Art. She had also gotten engaged to a young man whose name has never been revealed. Perhaps hoping to deter their daughter from pursuing a life in the theater, her parents told her she could audition for RADA—but only if she broke off her engagement. She had to choose whether she was going to commit to a career or a fiancé. Diana broke off the engagement.

"I came up to London, the city of sin, accompanied by Mrs. Greenwood and my mother," she recalled. The auditioning process was nerve-wracking. "You get four and a half minutes out there on stage to do one classical speech and one modern," she said. "I did a Catherine speech for my Shakespeare and I can't remember what I did for modern." Whatever it was, it worked. She was accepted, much to the dismay of her parents. However, despite their deep reservations, her parents offered at least financial, if not emotional, support. Beryl helped Diana locate a bed and breakfast in Kensington "run by a genteel lady who had fallen on hard times," Diana would later recall.

Suddenly finding herself on her own in London was a bit overwhelming at first, and Rigg admitted to *Cosmopolitan* that she felt at a disadvantage. "I was among a lot of people who seemed to know more about the theater than I did, but one had to *get on with it*, and it did make me a bit self-contained. Mine were not the sort of parents where I would talk about my lack of confidence."

Instead, Rigg put on a cloak of bravado and jumped into her new life with both feet.

CHAPTER TWO

• • • •

T H E Royal Academy of Dramatic Art has been a theatrical institution since the turn of the twentieth century when Sir Herbert Beerbohm Tree established the school at His Majesty's Theatre in the Haymarket. Tree, born Herbert Draper Beerbohm, is considered one of the great figures of English theater, probably as much for his business acumen as his acting skills.

Born in 1853, Herbert took the stage name Beerbohm Tree prior to his amateur debut in 1876. He turned professional two years later and became a well-known actor. In 1887 he leased out the Haymarket Theatre and set himself up as manager, which meant that he could cast himself in pretty much anything he wanted. And he did. Over the next decade, Tree portrayed every Shakespearean lead in productions that were as lavish as they were popular. The theater was such a great success that he built Her Majesty's Theatre and moved his operations there in 1897. He established a repertoire company that performed everything from poetic drama to children's shows, while his Shakespearean productions continued to play to packed houses. It seemed a natural progression, then, when he founded a school in 1904 that would become the Royal Academy of Dramatic Art. The school moved to its current location on Gower Street a year later, and students selected to join the company paid roughly the equivalent of ten dollars a term for the honor.

Tree was knighted in 1909 and the honor made his theater company that much more distinguished. Soon many notables of the day were recruited to sit on a managing council, including playwrights Sir Arthur Wing Pinero, Sir James Barrie and George Bernard Shaw. Three years after Tree's death in 1917, the school was granted a Royal Charter and became known as the Royal Academy of Dramatic Art, or RADA. Over the following years, through treasury grants and personal subsidies, the school was renovated and expanded, and at each new opening, a member of the Royal Family was there to christen each addition. When Shaw died in 1950 he left one third of all his royalties to RADA.

With the appointment of John Fernald as principal in 1955, RADA underwent some significant internal changes. Not only was the number of students admitted reduced but the standards for admission became far more stringent. The changes made RADA an elite and exclusive learning facility, but thanks to a system of government student grants, young actors without familial or personal means were still able to attend RADA. Among the first graduates to benefit from the grants were Albert Finney, Glenda Jackson and Anthony Hopkins.

By the time Diana Rigg walked through the august doors of RADA in 1955, the curriculum had evolved into a structured matrix intended to give an all-round theatrical education. According to the RADA Web site:

> During the first four terms a student concentrates on acquiring skills in voice, speech, phonetics, dialects, singing (group and solo), movement (including classes in the Alexander Technique), unarmed and armed combat. Classes, rehearsals or acting workshops constantly confront a student with the problems of acting: how to read a play, how to understand a playwright's intentions, to develop an imaginative response and communicate those intentions through the body and voice. Texts and scenarios from a variety of playwrights and periods are worked on in depth in order to give a sense of continuity and development of language and theatre practice.
>
> In later terms the balance begins to change, acting for television and radio is introduced and more time is given to extended rehearsal and performance in a very varied repertoire of plays for the public, professionally directed and designed.

When the term started, Diana met a shy girl named Valerie Pitts in the school locker room and the two seemed to naturally gravitate toward each other. Years later Valerie would marry famed conductor Georg Solti and become known as Lady Valerie Solti, who now says, "It felt very special in those days to have got a place at RADA. Diana and I had connection from the start because her parents lived in Leeds and my parents lived in Leeds."

Looking back, Rigg believes she entered RADA at an exceptionally vibrant time. Glenda Jackson and Sian Phillips were classmates, Albert Finney was ahead of them and the following year Susannah York was accepted. "Both Valerie and I went up at seventeen and were in a sense very much the same," Rigg told Jenny Gilbert during an *Independent on Sunday* interview. "We were both northern girls, deeply unsophisticated, though Valerie remembers me being able to handle it rather better than she did."

Lady Solti says that from the moment she showed up, Rigg "stood out from the crowd." She goes on to say, "She never manifested the blind funk that the rest of us felt. Even straight out of school she looked right, her makeup was right, she had poise. Her eyeliner was always done very expertly. She had red nail polish. She had this thick, naturally perfect auburn hair. Her voice was right. Everything was right. She denies this, of course."

Perhaps this shows just how good an actress Rigg already was because she remembers having to adjust to a completely new lifestyle. "There was so much to cope with: a big city, living alone and a course that one was ill-prepared for," she explained to Gilbert. "Leaving home to study was seen as rather a racy thing to do though in truth the ratio of boys to girls was pretty hopeless." At that time there was still the mandatory military draft, "so a lot of boys who might have wanted to act were doing that," Rigg said. "But in fact it didn't make any odds to us because Valerie and I were completely and utterly untouched by human hand and deeply naïve. We laugh about it now, in the light of what girls are like today. Ours were such innocent times. And our clothes were absolutely horrendous. Girls of our age were expected to dress like middle-aged women. I was sent away to London with three sweater-and-skirt outfits and that was it. We wore girdles, for God's sake."

However, the young Diana proved to be a quick study. Within a fairly short time, she began to discover the delights

London had to offer and found herself partial to the night life. Lady Solti recalls, "While the rest of us seemed to spend all our free time slogging away at our lines, Diana would go out to a party and spent thirty seconds the next day learning hers in the locker room and in class it would come out perfectly."

Living away from home and no longer under the yoke of her restrictive Moravian headmistresses, Rigg became more interested in experiencing life than studying the finer points of armed combat for stage. "Valerie by contrast was very contained," Diana admitted to the *Independent*. "On one occasion we took the same train home to Leeds and I remember her brushing her teeth furiously to get rid of the smell of cigarettes. I was rather blasé because my parents already knew I smoked. Valerie was a good girl in every respect, whereas I was nearly thrown out after our first year for not paying enough attention to my studies."

Although Rigg and her friends had little or no money, they still managed to have an active social life. They would frequently go see plays but stood in the back because they couldn't afford to buy a seat. They made do with whatever clothing they could pull together and in class often wore old oversized men's shirts, belted at the waist, over their tights. But even wearing what amounted to second-hand, thrift-shop clothes, Lady Solti says Diana's charisma was undeniable. "Among the rest of us it was Diana who had star quality. That extraordinary rich voice was there from the start. And getting one's voice right was what we all worried about. It had to be on the breath, centered, not too far back in the throat, not too far forward in your nose. You either spoke correctly or you didn't. If you had a few vowels that were not quite right, you worked at them." Ironically, Diana should have had the same issues correcting her speech as Valerie, but because she had grown up in India, where the English spoken was of the aristocratic kind, she never developed the harsh accent of the North.

Rigg once told *Photoplay* she did well her first year at RADA because, "Psychologically I was still at school." But the second year was different. "I became fully aware of being a young woman," she said. "I made friends, went to parties. In the second year I didn't do so well." Part of her rebellion had to do with the atmosphere at RADA. As she explains, "It was too rarefied. It had nothing to do with real life. As a matter of fact, I very nearly got thrown out because I was having a dose of real life on the outside."

After she completed her first year of studies, Diana moved out of her bed and breakfast and into an apartment in Hampstead with two roommates, an Australian and an American. "That's when my life began to be really rackety," Rigg admitted to the *Independent's* Gilbert. "This was pre-drugs, of course. We're talking cheap plonk and I suppose heavy petting, but that's as far as it went. You couldn't get away with much more. We had record players, but it was Chubby Checker dancing the twist and stuff like that."

Lady Solti mostly remembers the apartment for its parties—"an [awful] lot of parties." She explains, "And although I had digs on the other side of London, hers was always the place you'd go after an evening out when it was too late to get home. There was a sort of coal chute you could crawl through to get in and there would always be a sofa to sleep on. It was all fairly innocent, Diana had various boyfriends but one's private life was one's own in those days, and sex wasn't a thing any of us discussed. In many ways it was a more respectful society and certainly a lot safer and less threatening."

Rigg has fond memories of her bohemian days. She told the *Daily Telegraph* about her days living with an actress named Edna Landor: "I thought she was a lesbian, but she went on to have an affair with Paul Robeson. He was living at a place called Shottery Lodge and Edna would say, 'Paul wants me to hear his lines. Will you come with me?' So I used to sit in the kitchen at Shottery Lodge, with Paul's secretary, truly believing that Edna was in the bedroom hearing his lines. It's a wonderful euphemism, isn't it? I was so naïve."

She might have been naïve but she wasn't exactly a wallflower. And her extracurricular activities took their toll. In 1976 she told *Cosmopolitan*, "In my second year at the Royal Academy of Dramatic Art I made friends, I went to parties, I was not doing my homework. When I turned up in class I was half asleep because I had not been to bed the night before. Or I had been to bed but had not slept. I was not a good pupil. I didn't do so well academically."

But, despite the chronic tensions with the faculty, somehow Diana maintained enough equilibrium to avoid expulsion and finally got the chance to do what she had gone there for in the first place—to act. Rigg made her professional debut in 1957 as Natella Abashwili in *The Caucasian Chalk Circle* by Bertolt Brecht. The play was written in 1944 when Brecht was living in America, having fled Europe because of the war. He wrote the play for actress Luise Rainer, but she and Brecht had a falling out before the play could be produced. So instead of going to Broadway, *The Caucasian Chalk Circle* premiered as a student production at Carleton College in Northfield, Minnesota, in 1948.

In the RADA production, Rigg played the Governor's wife, who leaves her baby behind when she flees a political uprising. She later tries to get her son back from the peasant woman who has been raising the boy. In the end, a judge rules against Natella and leaves the boy with the woman who has proven herself to be the child's true, if not biological, mother. The moral Brecht intended to imply was that resources should go to those who will make best use of them.

The experience was exhilarating for Rigg. She told the *Daily Telegraph* in 1996: "It was the nicest feeling in the world. It was my first job and I had nowhere to go but up. Of course, I could have stayed at the bottom. But that's inconceivable when you're nineteen and full of natural optimism." Being on stage also brought Diana some self-realization. "One thing I learnt was that I had a special personal problem," she said. "Others have had it too. I would have to be the leading lady or nothing. Not a matter of ambition; a matter of physique. I was physically too big, too tall, to play juvenile parts, supporting roles."

Rigg managed to finish the term and squeaked out a diploma. "A pass. The minimum," she has happily reported in many interviews. Looking back, Diana seems less than enthused with her overall experience at RADA, saying the training "was not very comprehensive." She added, "I don't think it prepared one for the realities of making your way in theater." She went into more detail in a 1975 *New York Times* interview, saying the two-year course of study, "didn't mean a thing at that point, which means it could not get you a job in the theater." She went on, "I was never small enough or pretty enough to be considered the perfect juvenile. Wave that RADA diploma under the nose of some jaded theatrical figure and see what it gets you. Anyway you can't learn acting in drama school. You can learn the history of theater, costuming, make-up—but not acting. I suspected as much when I got there and it made me something of a less-than-satisfying student. And then I found the drama teachers revealing things like vocal blueprints for the sonnet. God! But then, when you have sixty raw students to start with, I guess it has to be a bit like a sausage machine, doesn't it?"

After leaving RADA, Rigg tried to get an audition with the Royal Shakespeare Company, but her overtures were rejected. To support herself, she took whatever jobs she could find, from being a clerk to answering phones. She also spent four months doing some modeling work. While her height might have been a drawback on stage, it worked to her advantage as a model. However, she never saw herself as true model material, which is why she always showed up for the shoots in casual, decidedly unfashionable clothes. "All the other models, of course, turned up well-groomed," she explained. "They were advertising themselves. The stuff I wore bore no relation to the fact I was a model." Which is why her modeling career was short-lived. "I turned up on a rainy day in a shapeless raincoat and Wellingtons and that was that as a model."

One of Rigg's top priorities after leaving RADA was to get

her Equity union card. So for eighteen months she did walk-on parts in two Yorkshire repertory theaters in Chesterfield and York. The Chesterfield repertory company offered Diana an apprenticeship that paid her seventeen dollars a week for doing a variety of jobs. In addition to acting, she worked as an assistant stage manager, which Rigg says, "ought to be essential to every actor's experience for what it teaches you about the pure mechanics of theater." She explains, "I was sent around the town to collect all the props. We had one sofa and two chairs and each Saturday, with tacks and glue, we'd re-cover the sofa for the next week's play."

Diana reveled being immersed in theater. However, at times she was perhaps a bit too enthusiastic. During one performance she prompted the actor so much, and so noticeably, that the local theater critic suggested in his column that she should have taken a curtain call. "I must have prompted seventy-three times," she told the *Sunday Times*. "I got a notice in the local Chesterfield newspaper, and none of the cast would speak to me."

Besides helping others with their lines, working in repertory helped her hone her own acting skills. "I am instinctive," she remarked. "I find it difficult to plod my way through a part, to sit down and say, 'scene three, she has reached such and such a point and would react this way.' In the course of reading a play to myself I get an instinct about the graph of the character, and playing develops the graph. One of the joys of long run is being able to develop. That's one of the joys and strengths of repertory, too."

In 1959, Rigg finally earned an audition with the Shakespeare Memorial Theatre, which today is known as the Royal Shakespeare Company and is located in Stratford-on-Avon, about an hour northwest of London. The theater had its beginnings in 1875 when a local brewer named Charles Edward Flower donated a two-acre parcel of land so a theater could be built in Shakespeare's hometown and the Bard's plays could be performed. The Shakespeare Memorial Theatre opened in 1879 with a performance of *Much Ado About Nothing* and had an initial season of eight days. In 1910, a month-long summer season was added, and fifteen years after that, the theater was granted a Royal Charter.

Over the following decades, the theater not only featured established Shakespearean actors but it also took an active role in training new generations of classical thespians. By the late 1950s, when Rigg auditioned, the company had gained international notoriety and had started going on international tours. For any British actor interested in furthering his or her classical career, the Shakespeare Memorial Theatre was the place to be. Rigg recalls waiting in a local church to hear whether or not she had been accepted. "I spent a lot of time in church in those days because it was the only place I could find that was warm and dry," she explained.

Like a lot of actors, Rigg was superstitious, and one day she had found a one-pound note in her purse she didn't know she had. She took her good fortune as a positive omen that success was only a matter of time. Her optimism was rewarded when she received word that she had been accepted into the company. Diana signed a three-year contract and, for the first time, felt that her career had finally started in earnest.

Chapter Three

• • • •

W H E N Rigg joined the Shakespeare Memorial Theatre, she couldn't know that the company was about to undergo an evolution. Not only did the name change in 1961 to the Royal Shakespeare Company, but starting in 1960, under the guidance of artistic director Peter Hall, the company was about to reinvent its self-image. He broadened the company's repertoire to include other Elizabethan dramatists as well as contemporary drama. "I was on the cusp of Glen Byam Shaw and Peter Hall's years," Rigg says. "Glen Byam Shaw went out with a bang. That year was Laurence Olivier, Paul Robeson, Edith Evans, Albert Finney and Charles Laughton. The following year there were stars, but that wasn't the main interest. Peter Hall had just begun to build his reputation as a director with the RSC and he was building an integrated company. He started a system of three-year contracts, which meant stability. I was being nurtured; I had the security and the knowledge that if I wasn't doing very much of this season, then next season I might. He made sure the walk-ons were given classes in voice and other disciplines. It was a tremendous foundation for the roles I graduated to." She has also frequently heaped praise on Michel Saint-Denis, who, she says, "taught us Chekhov, so when the time came and I got the part of Cordelia in Peter Brook's *King Lear* with Paul Scofield, and one of the leads in *Comedy of Errors*, I was ready."

But those roles were still far down the road. There's an old actors' cliché about beginning one's career as a spear-carrier with no lines, but for Rigg it was no hyperbole. Her first appearance in an RSC production was in *A Midsummer Night's Dream*. "I was playing an Amazon lady and I did actually have to carry on a spear," Rigg says wryly. She joined the company in 1959, the same year as Vanessa Redgrave, who was a year and a half older.

"I remember," Hall says, "an extremely good-looking girl glowering under her helmet on Hippolyta. She was very junior to Vanessa then and she didn't take over as Helena in *A Midsummer Night's Dream* until 1961. There was room for two of them because the company was expanding at the time and Vanessa left for a period to do other things. Diana was very easy to work with, very hard-working, terribly pretty."

In an interview with Michael T. Leech, she reminisced about another early role: "I was a walk-on in one of Tony Guthrie's productions at Stratford. It was a production of *All's Well That Ends Well*, with Dame Edith as the Countess. Zoe Caldwell was in it too, and Robert Hardy. [The designer] put me in pink, and I was one of the ladies of the court. Guthrie, who was absolutely wonderful at directing crowds, immediately started calling me the pink lady. 'Pink Lady, you do this,' or, 'Pink Lady, you go over there.' I don't think he ever learned my name.

"But Guthrie, you see, was a living example of care—he understood actors and he supervised things down to the very smallest detail. We all knew exactly what we were doing. It gave us all such a sense of purpose and one responds to that. Most directors just let you sort of mill around."

Along with fellow newcomers Vanessa Redgrave and Albert Finney, Rigg got to learn by watching living legends such as Dame Edith Evans, Paul Robeson and Laurence Olivier. Olivier was such an imposing talent that Diana says she would flatten herself against a wall whenever he walked by. "He was an astonishing man," she said. "He gave more to the theater than he ever got back." Later, Olivier in turn would call her "a brilliantly skilled and delicious actress," but at the time she had yet to graduate beyond understudy and walk-on roles. Even so, her now characteristic high-spiritedness was evident, causing Peter Hall to once comment, affectionately, that at the start of her career she was the rudest walk-on he had ever seen. Not everyone found her so endearing. Rigg had a tendency to burst out laughing with her trademark "Ha!" at inopportune moments. On one such occasion, Leslie Caron turned and snapped at Rigg to control herself: "Think of something sad, think of being fired!" Years later when she mused that while she had forgotten most of the Hindustani she had learned during her years in India, she did recall one phrase which was, "the equivalent of 'You are a son of a pig.'" She added, "I have found that to have its uses in the theater."

For every personal triumph, there seemed to be a painful learning experience. Rigg has said, "I was once so bad and uncomfortable in a part I became apologetic, which is to say I became inaudible, I guess. Someone in the stalls on opening night shouted a loud 'Speak up!' at me, so I learned that if you're going to be bad, go ahead and be bad. But be sure and be very grand and audible about it."

Rigg also recalls the freedom she felt when she met her first real challenge on stage. "I was an understudy at Stratford-on-Avon, when I was called on to replace the principal in *All's Well That Ends Well*," she said in an interview with Henry Gris. "Her name was Priscilla Morgan. They gave me maybe an hour's rehearsal. By a coincidence my parents were out front that night. I didn't tell them that I was going on, so that when I came out and started shaking they thought I was just walking on. Then they realized and sort of clutched each other in absolute fear.

"My fear was of a different kind. I was simply not sufficiently prepared and so I was annoyed with myself. Still, the audience was very kind, as it always is when an understudy takes over and doesn't want to make a complete mess of the play, and I was led forward and allowed to take a solo bow. I played it for about a week, I guess. And it was about the end of the week only that I began to enjoy it."

Although the experience she was getting was invaluable, her salary was meager. She was paid eighteen dollars a week, half of which went toward her rent. To make ends meet, she lived off woodpigeon (very inexpensive wild pigeon) scraps put inside intestines "that you can still get at the butchers' in the provinces—poor people's food." She went on, "Four times a week, my dinner would consist of that and maybe some potatoes and another vegetable, and fruit. And you know what? I was very healthy—and very happy." She also chain-smoked, which no doubt helped curb her appetite. But there was one luxury she refused to do without. "I could never do without perfume," she admitted to *TV Times*. "I guess I was so very young and this particular perfume was very heavy and musky and made me feel extremely sensual."

Diana remained a night person and enjoyed being invited to late dinner parties, going to the theater and making the round of discos. Rigg notes that for as intense as she could be on stage, she could be equally loose away from it. For example, she tended to forget her keys—repeatedly—and then would have to break a window—repeatedly—with a milk bottle to get back inside after a night out. "I don't pay much attention to details in my private life, and keys are not very important. My neighbor got tired of plastering in new panes of glass for me so he devised a window with a hinge and laid in a supply of glass." That way when she forgot her keys, she was able to fix the window herself.

On the nights she was home, Diana indulged in her favorite hobby—reading. Although she doesn't consider herself political, she discovered during the politically charged 1960s that her sentiments leaned toward the left, especially in matters of race. She once noted about the civil rights movement in America: "Blacks need security and background, not treacle."

For the girl raised in a strict religious school, being in the theater exposed her to lifestyles she had never heard of back in Yorkshire. "I had never even heard of homosexuality," she told the *Sunday Telegraph Magazine* in 1998. "My jaw dropped. I wasn't exactly hip in the sixties. I was too busy working fourteen hours a day. You had to drop out and wear beads and floaty things to be hip."

However, Rigg still found time for a social life. Now she freely admits, without getting into detail, that she had a number of lovers. "I was quite naughty in the sixties," she says. "Sexually free. That's what we could do. And we did it and I don't regret it for an instant. But I certainly wasn't boffing anybody in the company. I was a slow starter. All I wanted was to earn enough money to buy my father a bottle of whisky a week, and eventually I did."

After her spear-carrying debut and her appearance as Andromache in *Troilus and Cressida*, Rigg made her London debut in the RSC's 1961 production of *The Devils*, playing Philippe Trincant. Another small role in *Becket* earned Rigg ever more meaty appearances in productions at the company's Aldwych Theater in London: Helena in *A Midsummer Night's Dream*, Lady Macduff in *Macbeth*, Adriana in *The Comedy of Errors* and Cordelia to Paul Scofield's Lear in *King Lear*. "I was the tallest Cordelia in the world," the 5'9" Rigg has joked many times since.

While theater fed her soul, it didn't do much to put food on the table. To augment her meager RSC stipend, Rigg turned to television and was hired to do a guest spot on a series named *The Sentimental Agent*, in the episode called "A Very Desirable Plot," which aired November 23, 1963. The series was a spin-off from the popular *Man Of The World* and starred Argentinean actor Carlos Thompson as the owner of an import/export trading company in London who would find himself on the trail of criminals.

For Rigg, it was an easy way to make some quick money. Thompson, who was married to actress Lilli Palmer, was called by some the most handsome man in the world. Great things were expected of the series, which aired on Saturday nights. But however good his looks might have been, Thompson's English was barely passable and producers were forced to bring on a new character as an excuse to reduce Thompson's screen time. The series was cancelled after thirteen episodes and became a footnote in Rigg's filmography.

Rigg performed both *The Comedy of Errors* and *King Lear* in a touring company that traveled to Russia and the United States, where she made a surprising discovery: "Americans still didn't admit women to restaurants in a trouser suit. When I was in New York I was turned away at lunchtime." Obviously, they didn't know who she was. But back home, Rigg was getting noticed by her peers.

"Anyone who doesn't find her devastatingly attractive must be an Outer Mongolian monk," Douglas Fairbanks Jr. is reported to have said. Director Peter Brook compared her to Jeanne Moreau in a *TV Guide* interview. "She is a life, a medium soaking up a part so it speaks through her," he said. "She is what the French call a theater animal, one of those people with the theater in their blood. She likes night clubs and dinner parties but she is at the same time an intellectual who spends much time alone, reading, thinking, playing records." Even so, Diana would later admit, "I was not confident for many years playing the big parts at Stratford."

Her director for *King Lear* was Peter Brook, who was a pioneer of the British experimental theater movement and is considered by many to be modern theater's greatest innovator. He directed his first play when he was an Oxford undergraduate student. Brook alternated between theater and film, and his 1953 film *The Beggar's Opera* featured Laurence Olivier in his singing debut. A decade later he made *Lord of the Flies*, based on William Goldman's allegorical novel, as a brutal indictment of the British social structure. By 1964, his reputation preceded him at the RSC and Rigg admits she found herself wanting to entrust herself to him.

"Most actors and actresses at some point desire and feel the need for Svengali and it happened for me with Peter Brook," she said in a 1973 interview with Michael Kustow. "I felt he had what I needed. All you need is one man convinced of his power and one woman willing to place herself utterly and submissively in that power. So it worked rather well up until the final dress rehearsal, which, if I recollect all right, was at Stratford-on-Avon and went on until about three in the morning. I stayed behind afterwards and I said to Peter, 'It's not working, I can't do it. It's really not working.' 'No,' he said, 'you're right, it isn't.'"

Even though Rigg desired a Svengali, she couldn't compromise herself. She explained: "Inevitably one has to be absolutely, totally convinced that his ideas can fuse onto you, that the transplants can take place. I didn't, I rejected it. I deeply, subconsciously rejected it, so it didn't work at all. Nothing is more conducive to the truth than doing a dress rehearsal the eve of the first night. Peter gave me carte blanche to do more or less what I wanted, but I didn't have the courage. Round about the fifth week of playing, I hit on something and stuck to it and I couldn't move away or progress. It was a very limited sort of performance and I really was deeply apologetic. Peter is a very incredible man—very strong, utter, unquestioning belief—not my scene at all.

"I suppose I thought at that stage I would like to be a believer and found I could not. After that experience with Peter Brook, my attitudes towards a director changed. I suddenly realized that one had to contribute, that in fact one's survival depended on a contribution—mine did, anyway—and it was up to the director to simply select to lay it out. You don't present him with a blank sheet, like I did with Peter Brook. I felt under the spell of those baby blue eyes of his."

One of her last performances at the RSC before her contract expired was also one of her fondest memories of that period. It was a Royal performance given by command at Windsor Castle. Ever the hosts, the Royal Family made trays of champagne available offstage to any actor waiting to make his or her entrance and to "refresh" the actors between scenes. "It was one of the most spirited presentations of *The Comedy of Errors* we ever gave," Rigg recalls. She also reprised her role as Adriana in a national broadcast of *The Comedy of Errors* at the end of her tenure. Although Rigg had earned a reputation thanks to the RSC, when the company offered her a second contract in 1964, she declined. Part of it was a desire to travel a bit, and she took off to explore Europe and Canada. But part of it was no doubt because of the new man in her life.

Throughout her career, Rigg has been notoriously reticent about her private life. That inclination was probably cemented because her first serious, long-term relationship was with English film and television director Philip Saville. Saville, who began his career as an actor, was older, established and married. They lived together in the old studio of noted British painter Augustus John. When word of the relationship leaked out, it caused a bit of a stir, with the tabloids speculating on whether or not Saville would divorce his wife. In short order, Rigg adopted a rather flippant public stance on marriage, saying she had no desire "to be respectable." She told Paul Henniger of the *Los Angeles Times*, "I'm not available for marriage, no. But that doesn't mean to say that one's hardheaded or fantastically ambitious. Umm, it's not a philosophy I advocate for other people, but for myself I don't think the state of marriage is a particularly good idea." But this didn't mean she wasn't a proponent of monogamy. "I'm a one man woman. I'm faithful to the concept of marriage but not to the necessity of the sacrament itself. I'm happy and fulfilled and that's what counts, isn't it?" she said on other occasions.

Although Rigg told *Oui* magazine, "I've always been chary of marriage," she also admits her attitudes had undergone a change. "At seventeen, I dreamed of an early marriage and motherhood, but by the time I was twenty-two I didn't actually identify with it any more." Her attraction to Saville might be inferred from an observation she made to journalist Michael Kustow: "I find any man who is intellectually ahead of me attractive. That's the first thing that attracts me, actually. What is the second? Basically, how little he cares to exercise this power of his."

Although Saville lavished gifts on Rigg, such as a baby lynx jacket, she was still determined to be financially independent. Diana said that her goal, "generalizing on a vast scale, is to be free." She elaborated: "I want to be rich enough to do what I want. It's my eternal cry." So to that end, Rigg was more open to dabble in television than many of her RSC peers, much to the disapproval of those same peers.

Peter Brook went so far as to sniff, "If she doesn't waste herself on silly films, she could become something good."

Rigg was unconcerned. "Oh, she's wasting herself on television, she's wasting herself in films, and all that," Rigg recalled to Brett Thomas of the *Sun Herald* in 2002. "But now, everybody does it. They swap between media and that's the way it should be. The purists thought I should be a classical actress and only do classical theater. Rubbish!"

But little did Rigg imagine that her next television job would be the catalyst for her career taking a dramatic, and unexpected, turn. In late 1964 Diana appeared in the episode "The Hothouse" of *Armchair Theatre*, an anthology series that presented a different drama with a different cast every week. At the time only *The Avengers* was more popular. Around the same time, *The Avengers* then-current female lead, Honor Blackman, announced she was leaving the series to pursue a film career, having been cast as Pussy Galore in the next James Bond blockbuster *Goldfinger*. Producers did their best to change Blackman's mind but she couldn't be swayed, so auditions were held to find a new costar for star Patrick

Macnee. The new character's name was Emma Peel, and over sixty actresses were initially seen and tested. Months went by, and finally a beautiful actress named Elizabeth Shepherd was cast. But after seeing scenes from the first episode, the producers were not happy with Shepherd's performance. They abruptly stopped production of the next episode and let Shepherd go.

Casting resumed but nobody the producers saw seemed to have the right combination of qualities they felt Emma should have. Finally, Dodo Watts, who happened to be the casting director for both *The Avengers* and *Armchair Theatre*, suggested the producers bring in the young actress she had recently hired for "The Hothouse." They agreed, and television history was about to be made.

CHAPTER FOUR

•　•　•　•

W H I L E some modern viewers may assume that *The Avengers* was a small-screen offshoot of the James Bond films, the series actually debuted a year before the release of the first 007 feature, *Dr. No*. Sydney Newman, the Associated British Corporation's Director of Drama, called the series *The Avengers*. According to a Web site on the series, which can be found at www.theavengers.tv, Newman is quoted as saying, "I don't know what the fuck it means but it's a great title!"

With the premise and Hendry set, the network needed to find a compatible costar. Newman offered the job to Patrick Macnee. Although he was still relatively unknown, Macnee had been struggling to make a living as an actor for many years. Born in London on February 6, 1922, Macnee is the son of a kinswoman of the Earls of Huntingdon, who claim Robin Hood as an ancestor. His dad, Daniel "Shrimp" Macnee, was a famous horse trainer. But Patrick's upbringing was much more eccentric than outward appearances would have suggested. His dad was an alcoholic and his mother once took him to live with her rich lesbian lover named Evelyn, who eventually sent the boy away to school out of jealousy over his relationship with his mother.

As a young boy, Patrick grew up thinking he would be a jockey because he used to help his father train and learned to ride at an early age. "But I started to put on weight when I was sixteen so I decided to try something else," he says. For a while, that was gambling. He set himself up as a bookie while attending Eton and found he was rather good at it. "I was a successful one because I got tips straight from my father, then very active in the racing business," Macnee told Charles Bayne of *TV Times*. "I had two hundred pounds sterling in the kitty when the authorities caught me. I was nearly expelled."

So he gave up gambling and turned to the theater, playing Queen Victoria in the annual school play. After graduating, Macnee spent a year with the Bradford Repertory Company. He then came to London and appeared as Laurie in a production of *Little Women*. He also did some extra work on the film *Pygmalion* in 1938.

In 1941 he joined the navy and served as commander of a torpedo boat in the North Sea. When the war was over, Macnee returned to acting. Ironically, his riding expertise gave him a career boost. Producers of *The Elusive Pimpernel*, which starred Macnee's cousin, David Niven, needed an actor capable of riding a horse across the Loire River, and Patrick easily won the role. Although he worked steadily, Macnee never broke through to true stardom. So when he received a call from David Greene, who was working as a TV director in Canada, offering him a role in the series *The Moonstone* filming in Toronto, Macnee was open to relocating. "I was getting fair roles but nothing spectacular after the war," he told Robert Musel of the *Toronto Star Weekend Magazine* in a 1968 interview. Macnee says *The Moonstone* "was the first real break of my career. The years 1952 to 1955 were a wonderful time for TV in Canada. We opened the station in Toronto and did practically everything. Sidney Newman was head of the studio."

During the days, Macnee did radio to help pay the bills. He explains, "In retrospect, I was a very bad actor before Canada, very insular, very English. Radio helped my voice production and the roles I got on TV broadened my technique. I played with Lorne Greene and Christopher Plummer in *Othello* and with Lloyd Bochner in *Hamlet*."

Macnee made his way to California where he somewhat incongruously appeared in a series of westerns, including *Wagon Train* and *Rawhide*. "But that English accent was ridiculous," he noted wryly to Musel. Patrick returned to London after ABC-TV hired him to supervise the production for the series *Winston Churchill: The Valiant Years,* narrated by Richard Burton. So when Sydney contacted him about the role of John Steed, Macnee was initially hesitant, unsure if he shouldn't stay behind the camera. However, with no other producing work on the horizon, Macnee got over himself and accepted the role, at a salary of roughly $200 a week. "No one in Britain had heard of me," Macnee recalls. "I only got it because Sydney knew my work from Toronto."

With the cast set, the two-hour pilot was filmed, which would later be aired as two separate episodes. In the pilot, which was broadcast in January 1961, Keel's fiancée is murdered by a gang leader looking for his missing shipment of heroin. Vowing revenge for her death, Keel joins forces with Steed to successfully bring the gang leader to justice, which leads to Steed enlisting Keel as his permanent partner. However, it was clearly understood that the series' star was Ian Hendry and that Macnee was his sidekick, and in the first season, there were a couple of episodes in which Patrick did not appear.

Although Hendry's character was fairly well fleshed out from the beginning, in part because it was a reworking of his *Police Surgeon* role, Macnee's Steed was a virtual *tabula rasa*. Not surprisingly, in the pilot, Steed was nondescript both emotionally and visually. Macnee explains, "I'd been playing villains in three-cornered hats in Hollywood and I played John Steed the same way." Macnee recalls that Newman called him in for a meeting, saying, "Patrick, I'm afraid you're just not working out. You don't seem to *be* anything. Go away and think of something." Macnee took his inspiration from his father: "He was a horse trainer and a real dandy. He'd always wear big velvet collars, a cravat and a carnation in his buttonhole." So Macnee gave Steed an ultra-Edwardian fashion makeover, dressing him in perfectly tailored suits and a bowler hat, accessorized with an umbrella. The clothes complimented the old-world air Macnee adopted, which he said was merely "an updated version of Sir Percy Blakeney in *The Scarlet Pimpernel*." He added, "And I've been going on that way ever since."

According to Macnee, back when the show started it had been suggested his character carry a gun—a prop he forcefully objected to. "I said no," he explains. "I had been in the Second World War, and fighting and killing and seeing most of my friends being blown to bits. They said, 'What do you want to carry?' I said an umbrella as a joke! Let's not carry guns and give our school children ideas."

But for Macnee, the clothes reflected the personality he wanted to imbue Steed with. "Steed's things are light and flipperty-gibbet," he told *TV Times* in 1963. "They mean a lot but I can't give reasons for them. I've chosen my clothes on my own instinct completely. I love exceptionally wide cuffs. No good reason—except that I can wear enormous cuff-links. The pin-striped suit has been out of fashion for years, but they're fun to wear. My umbrella—nothing special about that, except that it must have a knobbly handle. I detest smooth handles. That's terribly important."

Macnee also channeled himself through Steed, living vicariously via the character's adventures. "In real life I am an adventurer. I fancy myself as a sort of Scarlet Pimpernel. I live by my own rules. I always have. Perhaps Patrick is not everything John is, but we are alike in many ways. Let's say Steed is a slightly exaggerated form of myself," he suggested in a 1961 *TV Times* interview. "Somebody once said to me, 'You should have lived in the eighteenth century.' I agree. Like Steed I'm a great pretender. Anybody who loves the good life as I do has to be a pretender."

Originally, *The Avengers* was filmed live, which Macnee found difficult because he tended to have a hard time learn-

ing his lines. To buy himself more time, he gave Steed a deliberate, almost languid way of talking. He also found the long
hours of filming an hour drama to be emotionally and physically draining. So to help the time pass and to keep himself
calm, Macnee drank. A lot. Patrick once told Steve Hocken-
smith of *Cinescape* that he and Hendry used to drink so much
"that when we watched [the show], the alcohol told us it was
terrific, but in fact I think it was pretty awful." Macnee said
nobody was concerned that the stars were never far from
a cocktail. "We all drank," he said. "At that age we never
thought of the future at all. I didn't stop until someone told
me that if I didn't, my liver might never recover. It did, but
look at Peter O'Toole. He's only got half a pancreas."

The more Macnee settled into the character and into the
grind of the series, the more his popularity among the viewers grew. Soon it was apparent to the producers, as well as
to Hendry, that there had been a role reversal—suddenly the
urbane Steed was the multi-dimensional character with the
huge fan base and by comparison, Hendry's dour Dr. Keel
seemed rather superfluous. When the producers decided that
pairing Steed with a female costar might lend even more zip
to the show, the decision was made to drop Hendry.

It was a surprising turn of events for Hendry, considering
the show began as a vehicle for him, the culmination of years of
single-minded dedication to acting. Unlike Macnee, who had
been pursuing acting since college, Hendry was a latecomer to
the theatrical party. Although he had a keen interest in acting,
after being discharged from the army Hendry had gone to
work as a real estate agent, opting for a steady paycheck over

following his heart's desire. He stuck it out for three years until his father finally intervened and offered to pay for Ian to attend London's Central School of Speech and Drama. His work in repertory theater led to small television guest roles, which in turn led to *Police Surgeon* and *The Avengers*.

The producers were apparently willing to write Hendry out gradually because in December 1961 the decision was made to keep his character on through the thirty-ninth episode while also introducing a new female partner to the team, a nightclub singer named Venus Smith. The idea was to have Smith's character alternate with Dr. Keel's. However, an Equity strike in 1961 shut down production at episode twenty-six and the series did not resume production for nearly a year. By that time Hendry had moved on to pursue other work. Over the years, Hendry worked steadily in films and on other series until his unexpected death at fifty-three on Christmas Eve in 1984. No cause of death was ever released.

For the first three episodes of the second season, Steed was partnered with Dr. Martin King, played by Jon Rollason, mostly to use previously written scripts intended for Ian Hendry. Although Julie Stevens was hired to play Venus Smith and Douglas Muir was brought on as One-Ten, neither were intended to be the yin to Steed's yang. It wasn't until co-producer Leonard White created the character of Cathy Gale and hired Honor Blackman to play her that Steed finally found a truly compatible partner.

Later, Diana Rigg would reveal that although the decision had been made to give Steed a female partner, in the script the character had originally been written as a man. "And although

Honor Blackman took it over, the basic attitudes and capabilities of the character were never changed for a woman," Rigg told *Oui* in 1975. She added to Carolyn McGuire of the *Chicago Tribune* ten years later: "They just sort of dressed her in black leather and let her get on with it. She had a lot of what would have then been considered masculine attributes. The writers sort of fell into this advanced woman. They didn't think it out."

One of the more refreshing aspects of British television, from the 1960s through today, is that it's not just filled with perky twentysomethings. While Britain certainly had its share of starlets, in part a reaction to Hollywood's youth push, there seemed to be room as well for more mature sensibilities. When Honor Blackman was cast in *The Avengers*, she was in her mid-thirties and mostly known for her captivating voice—which, truth be told, she worked hard to develop. When Blackman was fifteen, her father gave her a choice between getting a bicycle and having voice and diction lessons. "We came from the East End and my vowels were practically nonexistent," she told the *Evening Mail* years later.

"My father was very much aware that in those days if you wanted to make the grade you had to speak like a lady," she explained. "I hadn't been allowed to have a bicycle because my sister had a fearful accident and nearly died. I think I did want that bicycle. It would have been a lovely prize. It was something I had never been allowed to have—now it was in my grasp. But I think he knew that I really wanted to be an Eliza Doolittle and change my speaking; not that I was as bad as Eliza, I hasten to add. So I went to a lady in Bournemouth.

She was quite wonderful and very inspiring. You have to learn on something, though; you just can't read the telephone directory. So she gave me little scenes from plays and poetry to learn." And that was when Blackman became enamored of acting. The plays she was given transported her to a world she didn't know existed. She recalled, "In what was laughingly called my schooling, I don't think I had ever heard of Shakespeare. I don't think he was ever mentioned in my life. I was totally ignorant of that part of the world. The theater. Everything." Although she enthusiastically pursued acting, she did so not really believing it was something you could make a living at. "It still surprises me today that I am here doing things I love and having lots of fun, that it is actually called work," she commented.

As so often happens in television, Blackman was not the original choice of the producers for the role of Cathy Gale. Sydney Newman wanted Nyree Dawn Porter, who had previously guest-starred on the series, but when she was unavailable, Blackman was hired instead, somewhat against Newman's better judgment. He thought her acting style was too proper and soft-edged and he warned her early on that if she played Gale that way, she would be out of work sooner than later. So Honor accepted the challenge and the result was a spirited, liberated, self-sufficient Cathy Gale, a character who in retrospect was stunningly ahead of her time. Blackman was fond of saying: "I'm a first for television—the first feminist to come into a television serial; the first woman to fight back."

As the character evolved, so did the emphasis on hand-to-hand fighting skills, which Blackman wanted to be genuine.

"You've got to have realism," Honor explained at the time. "Televiewers are so perceptive they instantly spot mistakes and write in to complain." She told the *Manchester Evening News* that she had taken lessons from a London hotel proprietor who was once in the French Resistance. "He taught me how to throw an assailant and one or two other little tricks used in France during the war. Some of them were much too tough to be used on TV."

However, Macnee did not share her enthusiasm for realism. "I've always been completely unphysical," he said. "I was forced to play games at school but I never enjoyed them. All that stuff about people doing their own stunts is rubbish. You're paid enormous amounts of money by the insurers *not* to do them."

A bigger issue for Blackman was that people wanted to challenge her skills in person. "Too many people want to try me out!" she explained. "I'm terrified one day I shall come unstuck. After all, I'm only a yellow belt—one of the lowest grades. It only needs a black belt to give me a going-over and I'd never work again!" As it was, Honor admitted, "I collect plenty of bruises from the studio falls—though fortunately where they will never show!"

The emphasis on hand-to-hand necessitated a change in wardrobe—flinging bad guys over your head is not particularly dignified when wearing a dress. So it was serendipity that Blackman started a new fashion craze when she suited up in leather—a turn of events Macnee took credit for in a *TV Times* interview: "It started off in the simplest sort of way. I love leather and it's tough and hard-wearing. Then it won popularity because such a hard, tough material on a soft, white skin obviously has a stunning effect." He adds that any insinuations at "kinkiness" were deliberate.

However, others say the leather outfits came about for more practical reasons—after Blackman bent over in a fight scene and completely ripped open the back seam of her pants. But with the leather came a new fashion statement. According to Blackman: "The only things you can wear with leather trousers are boots, so they kitted me out with calf-length black boots and the leather thing was born."

But for all its evocative virtues, leather could also be restricting. So during her second season, London fashion designer Frederick Starke was hired to create a new leather wardrobe, as well as some pseudo-leather pieces for fight scenes. Starke explained in a 1963 *TV Times* interview that this faux leather has "more stretch in the material." He added, "Leather doesn't give much, and with Cathy being thrown about and throwing people about, it could split." It was Starke's job to give her an appropriate wardrobe that was equally classy. "Cathy is meant to be a fashionable woman," he said. "She can wear anything so long as it isn't fluffy. She is a beautiful girl with a lovely figure, but an unusual bone structure makes her difficult to fit."

The combination of Macnee's Steed and Blackman's Gale turned a mildly popular series into a bona fide television phenomenon in Britain. The sexual innuendo, the campy scripts and the then-new, uncharted cultural role reversal—having a kick-your-ass female with a dandyish male partner—gave the series a unique point of view that fit snugly in the pending cultural shifts of the mid-1960s in Swinging London. "*The Avengers* really gave women a dignity and strength," Macnee observed to the *Independent* in 1997, "if only on a comic-strip level." But he doesn't think the strength of Gale, and later Mrs. Peel, diminished Steed: "He wasn't submissive but equal. I just let the women get on with it, but I don't think it made me less of a man."

For all the notoriety and popularity Macnee and Blackman enjoyed, they were prevented from fully capitalizing on it, either professionally or financially. Their salaries were modest, even by standards of the time, but more disheartening was the short leash the producers kept them on. "We weren't even allowed to do commercials," Macnee recalled to the *Independent*. "The producers said it would demean the series. I don't know why they were so precious; the first reviews we got said, 'The commercials are slightly more amusing and interesting than the show itself.'" When Macnee asked for a percentage of profits, he says he was told, "We don't need you that much, Patrick—we'll just get a younger man." Macnee explains, "The management called us The Talent but treated us like chimney sweeps."

The Avengers was such a hit in England that it caught the interest of Hollywood. Toward the end of Blackman's second season in December of 1963 a U.S. producer approached the Associated British Corporation about turning the series into a feature film. Not to be outdone, a Broadway producer floated an idea of turning *The Avengers* into a theatrical musical. But whatever excitement these offers generated was abruptly doused when Blackman told producers she wouldn't return for a third season. There has been much speculation as to why exactly she would leave a show just seeming to hit its stride. But in a 2000 interview with Fred Norris of the *Evening Mail*, Honor says it was simply time to go. "Right at the beginning I said I would go after a certain length of time," she explains. "I don't worry about being typecast, but the thing is not to stay so long you forget what you can do. But I also thought two years was long enough, although I must say they were all terribly surprised and shocked that I did leave. I think I was right. I wasn't right financially. I could have made a lot more in the series but I have no regrets at all. I have never thought it right to grade everything in terms of money. Life for me is not like that."

Blackman's series finale was a carefully guarded secret. To keep the circumstances of her character's departure from leaking to the press and public, the script was intentionally left unfinished, leaving off just as Cathy is trapped inside a burning boathouse, with flames engulfing the camera. But of course, she survives and the episode ends with her saying good-bye to Steed before leaving for the Bahamas, never to return.

Blackman, on the other hand, was going from one high-profile job directly to another. She had been cast by Albert "Cubby" Broccoli to costar in his next James Bond extravaganza, *Goldfinger*, in the sought-after role of Pussy Galore, earning a $20,000 payday. "She's bad, of course, and she's tough," said Honor. "In fact, I'll be taking a lot of Cathy Gale with me. I expect that was why I was chosen for the part." Although it's often inferred that Honor left *The Avengers* to appear in the film, she had already announced her intention to quit prior to the film offer. While the move might have been timely for Blackman, it appeared for a while as if it would also be the premature death of *The Avengers*. With their female lead gone, the ABC abruptly pulled the plug and ceased production of the series while they figured out how to proceed, or even if they should proceed.

Macnee waited patiently, having no interest in following Blackman's lead and trying to parlay his small-screen popularity into a feature-film career. "I never had what it takes to be a star," he said candidly years later. "I got too secure in that role. By the end I looked upon myself and the public with scorn. If you get too complacent, you're sunk."

In the end, *The Avengers* was sold to Telemen Limited, which recruited Albert Fennell and Brian Clemens to become the show runners. And the two set out to see if they could relaunch the show with a new actress. They would have never dreamed that lightning was about to strike twice.

CHAPTER FIVE

• • • •

R A T H E R than try to recast the role of Cathy Gale, they decided it was more prudent to bring in a completely new character but one that would essentially pick up where Blackman left off—in other words be just as liberated and liberating as Gale. During the audition process, the character was tentatively called "Samantha," until the show's new publicist, Marie Donaldson, came along and decided Steed's partner needed a flashier, and insinuating, name to highlight the character's "man appeal." From that, Donaldson came up with "M appeal," which resulted in "Emma Peel." The thumbnail description of Mrs. Peel was that she was the widowed wife of a test pilot and the chairman of Knight Industries, founded by her father, Sir John Knight.

Among the actresses who auditioned for the role was Diana Rigg. At the time her television experience was limited to her appearance in "The Hothouse," and she had just returned from touring with *King Lear*. "I didn't know the program because I didn't have a television and it was touch and go whether I went to the audition," she later recalled. "It did not seem to be me, somehow. In the end though, I went for a giggle. The studio was overrun with incredibly ambitious young women jostling to get the part and I never expected to get it. We were asked to wear black sweaters and pants and the assembled group looked like a neo-fascist army. And afterward I said to one of the producers, 'This is all a waste of time, isn't it?' The producer agreed with me." Rigg was so convinced she had no chance to be hired that she admitted in an interview with Peter Calder that she showed up late for her callback for a second audition: "I'd gone off to have lunch with a friend who lived nearby and we had a few glasses of wine and they were a bit cross with me."

After two months of searching, producers finally chose twenty-eight-year-old Elizabeth Shepherd, another blonde who, unlike Blackman, was in the beginning of her career. Macnee was generous in his approval: "I am delighted that she has been chosen. She is very beautiful."

The daughter of a minister, Shepherd approached acting with a decidedly blue-collar work ethic. "I spent my childhood in Burma, and my life was far away from the theater, but it had many things in common," she once told the *Toronto Star*. "I was brought up to think of work as a vocation. My father was a preacher and would bare his heart and soul in front of a congregation, so it ran in the family."

In addition to a new female lead, the show was undergoing other significant changes. Instead of being shot on video tape, it was now going to be filmed, which meant that the series was no longer tied to a sound stage, which meant increasing the aesthetics of the series by being able to shoot on location. Macnee was directed to imbue Steed with even more stereotypical upper-crust British mannerisms. And the fantasy element was subtly honed. "Because we were a fantasy, we have not shown policemen . . . and you have not seen anything as common as blood," producer Brian Clemens said in a 1969 *TV Times* interview. "We have no social conscience at all."

The idea was to create a fantasy world in which the most bizarre, fantastic or surreal stories could seem plausible. Whereas the series might have started as a drama-spy thriller hybrid, as time went on it became more fanciful, a place where deadly man-eating plants were as much a potential foe as a robot from outer space. Dreaming up the story lines was an adventure unto itself. "My own technique, when I thought of an idea, has been to dream up twelve good dramatic moments and lead in and out of them," explained Clemens. "I must have twelve for a fifty-minute script. If I'd only got six I was only halfway there. And this series chewed up scripts at the rate of one every ten days."

With so much emphasis on creating such a special world, the series' art director, Bob Jones, was under constant pressure to realize the vision of the writers without breaking the budget. Jones noted: "I've been in films and TV since 1953, but when I first came to *The Avengers* . . . I felt as though I'd never worked so hard in my life. Now I'm used to it, but it needs a very special mental approach." That's because everything needed to have a surreal bend. "If it was a solicitor's office the chap couldn't be an ordinary solicitor," Jones explained. "We'd have him ride a bicycle round his desk, or make him a collector of top hats—hundreds of 'em. I'd say to a writer: 'What's this chap's background? Let's make him quite mad—have him live in a tube station.'"

"It was both a dream and a nightmare for an art director because every idea you thought of nearly always had to be a working model," says Jones. "I've had Steed drop down a manhole into an underground room decked out as a faithful reproduction of The Oval cricket ground at Kennington in 1880, with wickets, pads—the lot. I've designed a bathyscaphe—that bubble thing that takes you down to the sea-bed—its interior completely equipped and decorated as a Georgian parlor. I've built a complete death factory, computer-programmed to kill agents. There were about forty ways of dying, and each one had to work."

Because the show did not have the luxury of time to school Shepherd in the requisite martial arts, she was taught each episode's fight sequences by the series' instructor, Ray Austin. But shortly after filming of the second episode, "The Murder Market," began, Shepherd was abruptly fired. Director Peter Graham Scott would explain that "the scenes with Beth Shepherd hadn't got any fire in them." Macnee backed the director up, noting in his book *The Avengers and Me*, "Beth Shepherd as Emma Peel was a square peg in a round hole."

Shepherd herself would later admit to the *Toronto Star* that her penchant for rewriting scenes and dialog probably hastened her departure. "They said they welcomed my ideas for Emma—those were fatal words," she explained. "So I inundated them with wonderful ideas, many of which appeared in the series: I said Emma would have to do karate. They said it would show in her hands, but I said she always wore gloves, she had a gloves fetish. In the second episode, they terminated my contract."

It was an expensive decision because it meant having to scrap an episode and a half. The production would be pushed further behind schedule as the producers went back to take a second look at the previous audition tapes. This time, they found themselves particularly intrigued with an actress who had previously slipped under their radar. As one of the producers, Julian Wintle, explained, "Her animal quality stuck in our minds." After viewing a tape of the play, the producers called Rigg back to do a screen test with Patrick Macnee. Rigg's magnetism, along with her chemistry with Macnee, won her the part, about which Diana noted, "I didn't know what I was in for except I knew the lady fought."

And just like that, she was starring in one of the most popular series in Britain—much to the shock and dismay of her theater peers. Although actors today float between film, TV and theater as a matter of course, back in the 1960s many theater actors sniffed at small-screen work as being somehow inferior to the "real" acting of the stage. Rigg shrugged off the disapproval, joking, "It was a perverse decision in a long line of perverse decisions." On a more serious note, she told the *New York Times* in 1966, "I decided to try and become commercial for a change. The trouble with staying with a classical company is that you get known as *a lady actress*. No one ever thinks of you except for parts in long skirts and blank verse."

Later, she would add in *Time*, "They want to box me up, frame me and put a title under me, but I defy that. I'm both a commercial *and* classical actress. Besides, it doesn't matter what you do as an actor. We started as vagabonds, playing in churches, barns and halls. I'm only tramping the same route. Of course, I could end up a jack-of-all-trades and master of none. But then, to be a master of one would spell infinite boredom." Plus, she added, "If you care about the theater, you can feed new audiences into it from television."

Jumping boots-first into production, Rigg set about making Emma Peel her own. Thanks to all her theater training, and her lanky frame, the physicality of the role seemed to come naturally to Diana. Reporters invited to watch her train were treated to seeing Rigg flip her martial arts trainer, Ray Austin. "I enjoy the rough stuff," Rigg told the *Daily Mail*. "It's fun knocking people about and getting paid for it." Her enthusiasm prompted Macnee to muse: "I'm glad she's on my side. I wouldn't want to be on the receiving end."

Rigg and Macnee's styles melded smoothly together, and they shared a similar view of their characters. "Patrick and I chose a very tongue-in-cheek approach. That made it more fun for us and more believable for the audience," Rigg said.

In *The Complete Avengers* by Dave Rogers, Macnee recalled, "The scenes we played together, with the full approval of Brian Clemens, were largely rewritten by Diana and myself and I thought they were quite funny! She had a very sharp and lively imagination and understanding of what a woman, a woman like her, would say in any given situation—however outrageous or mad. We took perfect straight situations and

Rigg's role on *The Avengers* required a variety of exotic—and revealing—costumes

made them slightly ludicrous. You had to be slightly mad, but also basically cool. We tilted everything, made it humorous, and it worked!" Macnee also said, "She was the man, I was the woman."

However, while Rigg certainly played Emma as a self-assured, self-sufficient woman—she's always called "Mrs." because "it shows she knows what it's all about"—she also noted to *TV Guide* in 1967, "Emma Peel is not fully emancipated. Steed pats me from time to time like a good horse." Rigg would also later note that although the character, which was simply a renamed and reworked version of the Honor Blackman character, which in turn had been originally written for a man, Emma was made dependent on Steed. "If you noticed, I was never really a serious threat to the fellows," she said. "I'd spend half a shooting fighting off three stuntmen, for example, and then Steed would come along and demolish them all with one stroke of his umbrella." Revealing a bit of her subversiveness, Rigg also noted: "I wanted to be Lady Peel, not for any grandiose reasons, but simply because it seemed to get some rather good comments over on the English aristocracy. Of course they wouldn't do it."

As to their characters' offscreen lives, Rigg said, "My physical relations with him are, to put it mildly, ambiguous. They're certainly not active on the screen but I don't think they did have an affair. I think it was one of those relationships where the promise that they might be in the future sustained it." She described it to Vince Cosgrove as "one of those glorious, deeply intimate flirtations that spin off into infinity."

Macnee, on the other hand, frequently made the case that Steed and Peel were lovers. "Definitely. I should say they slept together at least three or four times a week," he once boasted to *TV Guide*. "The adrenaline of excitement always leads to sex. What would be very worrying is if we hadn't gone to bed. Can you imagine Emma Peel in a leather suit and Steed not going to bed with her? They just didn't make a song and dance about it. The sixties were wonderful for putting sex in its place. It was taken much more for granted after the forties and fifties when everyone wondered what the other person looked like without clothes on." He maintains that showing them in an intimate clinch would have ruined the tone and electricity of the show. "We're each there separately for the audience, not for each other," he added to the *New York Times*. Each episode is "erotica spaced out between tensions."

While Macnee might have wanted to spur speculation among the viewers, producer Wintle brushed off the issue by saying, "They are *not* sleeping together."

However, it seemed that half of the U.K.'s male population would have lined up at the opportunity. Part of the prurient interest was because of Rigg's striking physicality, part a reaction to the intentional titillation included in the scripts. In one case, the writers truly outdid themselves and earned the scrutiny of the Independent Television Authority, or ITA, which had been established by Parliament in 1954 to oversee commercial broadcasting in Britain. The ITA, which later was called the Independent Broadcasting Authority, ordered producers to either edit a minute out of the episode "A Touch of Brimstone," in which Emma Peel was apparently being whipped, or change the broadcast time to after 9:00 P.M. Rather than change the schedule, the offending scene was excised.

According to Rigg, Emma Peel was the conduit for some of the writers' personal predilections: "That show catered to every kinky thing imaginable—and no wonder, considering some of the writers we had. We had a foot fetishist I'll never forget. That's why I was always being photographed in leather boots with my feet stuck in the air somehow. Another one was fascinated by bondage, so for another string of shows I was always getting tied up in some outlandish way. And the leather! God, I thought I'd never get out of all that leather."

Ironically, despite the risqué content, psychiatrists named *The Avengers* the best "non-corrupting" program for children. Rather refreshingly, in light of the tight grip of political correctness that pervades U.S. airwaves, Steed and Peel's fondness of alcohol wasn't considered "corrupting." As it happens, that was one trait Rigg and her small-screen alter ego shared. "I'm always very well stocked," she told Henry Gris, "but I never drink it at the studio. The stuff Patrick Macnee and I drink on camera is bubbly lemonade, very harmless. I don't touch the stuff then. You mustn't when you work. At home, well, that's another story."

Seeking to capitalize on the show's popularity, producers started a clothing franchise of *Avengers* clothing and accessories, designed by John Bates, Alun Hughes and others. Contrary to popular lore, Rigg did not regularly wear leather on the show, finding it too constricting, although she did occasionally wear leather for certain scenes, despite its being impossible to maneuver in. "With my tight leather suits on, I always had terrible difficulty getting out elegantly," she told *Vanity Fair's* Mark Ginsburg, referring to the Lotus Elan she drove in the series. "You could just stand up, vaguely bend—no vaulting possible." Instead, she preferred form-fitting knits and dresses. Hughes gained notoriety by designing the "Emmapeeler," the slinky crêpe cat suits Rigg wore when the series transited to color, which Hughes claimed were good for both work and leisure.

During the second, or color, season, producers did make Rigg wear another leather costume in response to viewer letters lamenting the lack of leather. However, the $800 outfit, designed by Alun Hughes, met an untimely death. Worn in the "You Have Just Been Murdered" episode, the outfit was ruined while filming the stunt sequences, suffering several seam splits.

Rigg herself also contributed to *The Avengers'* fashion legacy by promoting the then-risqué miniskirt. "The designer and the other men were horrified," she admitted to *TV Times*. "They pulled their hair, said, 'You can't do that, it's impossible.' I argued that one must look forward and not back, and by wearing these brief skirts, one was looking forward. In fact, one was creating fashion very avant-garde, rather than remaining at the tail end of last year's styles. And it turned out that I couldn't have been more right." However, she wasn't a public fashion plate. "I never wear the clothes in the series outside," she said. "But there's a style there that I think is common to both of us, and I have no intention of changing my appearance after Emma Peel is no more. After all, it was I who affected her."

But for all the sexiness and erotica emanating from and surrounding Emma, the true strength, and appeal, of the character was the perfect convergence of the right actress playing an innovative role on the cusp of a cultural revolution for an audience craving something unique and fresh. Gerard Gilbert of the *Independent,* wrote: "It was her demeanor that was so ground-breaking in a television landscape where attractive young women were mostly game-show dolly birds. This woman could high kick as well as deliver droll repartee, and if Steed had occasion to rescue her, she delivered herself ironically to her white knight. Rigg suggested that intelligence, as well as leather, could be sexy, in an age when baby-doll nighties and false eyelashes were the mainstream alternative." It's no wonder that when girls from a South London youth club were asked who they'd like to lecture them on poise, Diana Rigg was the first choice.

Macnee also had his admirers. Michael Billington of *The Stage and Screen Today* wrote: "Patrick Macnee's Steed is by now unimprovable. One's only regret is that he has not had more chance to exploit his comic timing and thoroughbred appearance outside this particular series. Opinions about Diana Rigg's performance are divided. I feel that she has made a definable character of Emma Peel, something without much help from the scriptwriters. And whatever her costumes—last week she was a strikingly clad Queen of Sin—she has looked constantly fetching."

For as much as the forty-five-year-old Macnee reveled being in the spotlight after decades of surviving as a struggling actor, Rigg was taken aback by the attention. "It was odd, suddenly having everybody recognize you," she said. "I gave out autographs for a while and then decided to stop. I was working one day when a group of holiday makers approached me for an autograph. I refused and they started booing and hissing. I was terrified. I started writing my name immediately and now I give autographs, though I don't comprehend exactly why people want them. I simply don't understand the autograph syndrome." While she might have been cowed into being responsive to requests for her signature, she wasn't intimidated by fan mail and would leave bags of it unopened.

However, not everyone was impressed. The *Daily Mirror* trumpeted a challenge issued to Rigg by a sixteen-year-old girl named Christie Wildman who held a black belt in judo. "If anyone tried the sort of throw Diana uses in the role of Emma Peel, she would end up flat out," Christie sniffed. "The throws in *The Avengers* aren't realistic. They are faked." Just in case Rigg actually entertained a notion to take Wildman on, a spokesman for the British Judo Association issued her a warning: "Christie is a judo natural. It often takes big men five years to win the black belt."

Not only was *The Avengers* a pop-culture hit in Britain, it was a hit throughout Europe and beyond, having already been sold to fourteen countries. It also happened to be an extremely expensive show to produce thanks to its ever-changing sets, costing over $600,000 per episode. Although the foreign rights brought in some extra revenue, the most coveted market was the U.S., primarily because it was also the most lucrative. Although both NBC and CBS passed when approached by Howard Thomas, managing director of ABC Television Ltd., ABC—which is not affiliated with the British ABC—was interested. But the American network had serious reservations about buying a show shot in black and white. So a compromise was reached: if ABC bought the first season of the show in black and white, the second season of *The Avengers* would be delivered in color.

The news made headlines in Britain. The *Times* reported: "*The Avengers* has been sold to the American Broadcasting Company. . . . A sum of over $1 million is involved. The sale is the outcome of a recent visit to New York by Mr. Thomas and Mr. Robert Norris, newly appointed director in charge of A.B.C.'s television film interests. 'I have no doubt it is only the beginning,' Mr. Thomas said."

For all the excitement the sale generated, there was also concern whether or not the show would translate to the American audience. Although Howard Thomas would publicly proclaim, "We have not made any concessions for the American market. The Americans like it because it is different and sophisticated," the fact was, adjustments were made. The most obvious was the agreement to start producing the show in color for the second season. The more immediate change was the new introduction shown at the beginning of the episode. Originally, the opening sequence had John Steed telling Mrs. Peel they were needed and off they would go to start the episode. However, when the show premiered on ABC in March 1966, the opening showed a man with a champagne bottle in his hand—and a knife in his back—collapse onto the ground, which is revealed to be a chessboard with life-sized

game pieces. Steed and Peel enter into the picture. Macnee takes the champagne bottle and they drink a toast before leaving to start their adventure. So that there was no mistake about the premise, the brief "we're needed" dialogue was replaced by the following monolog: "Extraordinary crimes against the people and the state have to be avenged by agents extraordinary. Two such people are John Steed, top professional, and his partner, Emma Peel, talented amateur—otherwise known as The Avengers." To further woo the American audience, well-known guest stars, such as Donald Sutherland and Christopher Lee, were cast.

Although it wasn't uncommon to "import" foreign series and adapt them for the American audiences, using American actors and tweaking the setting to Americanize it, the success The Avengers enjoyed in the U.S. was unique in that it was a British series starring British actors. Although other series, such as Monty Python or Fawlty Towers, would find cult success, The Avengers was a prime-time hit for a major broadcast network. Not only was it a popular hit, it was a critical success as well, earning Emmy nominations for Best Drama Series in 1967 and 1968. Rigg also earned a Best Actress nomination in 1967, but lost to Mission Impossible star Barbara Bain.

Macnee heaped praise on his costars, telling TV Times, "It's all due to the girls. Two completely independently-minded, absolutely wonderful females have been the success of The Avengers—or at least a great part of it." He also gave the credit to the production itself. "We do it quite differently," he told the Los Angeles Times in 1968. "Often we work on two shows at once, and we spend a minimum of ten days on each one. In

America, they spend at the most seven days and never start over again. We once threw out a whole show and did it over again. If you do an adventure show, you can't do it well in eight days. We took much longer to make them. Here everyone wants to become a millionaire; I think they need to take time, and not be as greedy. I think the show is consistently good because they use good directors and some of the most imaginative writers in Britain. The writing and direction are terribly important in a show like ours."

Rigg agreed. "The difference is between getting involved in ludicrous situations and making a comment on them, which I think is a mistake," she said in a 1967 *Los Angeles Times* interview. "One should, at the same time, be able to keep a level of awareness so that you can bring as much comedy within this ludicrous situation as possible without actually setting yourself or the situation up." As far as why U.S. television viewers were so enthralled with the show, Rigg lopped the kudos back to her costar: "Patrick has been marvelous. The series has been successful, I think, because we have broken away from the stereotype. We have inverted the usual ideas and added humor to the inversion."

Brian Clemens thought the key to the series' U.S. success was it gave the American audience something truly unique. "We became terribly British," he said. "A car is a car is a car, and not an automobile. A lift is a lift is a lift, never an elevator. It is this Britishness that fits the fantasy world so appealing to the Americans." Producer Wintle added simply: "They like Steed's courtesy in the U.S."

Actually, what they liked was Emma Peel. *Newsday* wrote

that Rigg's casting "couldn't have been a better choice, particularly in the minds of male fans. As one chap put it, 'Give a man a pudding and Diana Rigg during the lunch hour and experience shows he will be a thing of slobbering contentment from start to finish.'"

Playboy was equally as rapturous: "But the star is definitely Diana Rigg, who, as the widowed Mrs. Emma Peel . . . exudes more sheer sexuality than American TV has previously handled. Mrs. Peel is an erotic stylization, rather than a character, in pants suits, miniskirts and an incredibly kinky wardrobe. Her other great attribute is that she is one of the neatest brawlers anywhere: she karate-chops villains by the roomful, barely mussing her leather fighting suit. There are no holds barred for Miss Rigg or for the show's uproarious style. It's all high-wire melodrama, good-humoured fetishism and flamboyant self-mockery. We hopefully expect it to be with us for a long while."

Rigg seemed bemused by the hoopla. "We're very pleased about that, delighted and rather surprised, especially on the basis of its being an English series without any sort of compromise toward making it an English-American product." Although she was pleased with the series, she wasn't a fan of TV in general or watching herself in particular. "I don't watch television at all except for occasional documentaries," she explained. "Instead, I read a lot." While working on the series, she only watched two of the episodes. "Everything, to me at least, is transparent. I can see the workings of my mind, the technique. I know too much about myself to find myself particularly attractive," she remarked.

Because of the changes made to export *The Avengers* to America, the show's survival was now completely dependent on the American revenue it received. But just as the producers were gearing up for the color season, Rigg dropped a bombshell.

CHAPTER SIX

• • • •

IF there has been a credo Rigg has followed in her professional life, it's to avoid complacency. That mindset was a factor, at least in part, of her decision to accept the role of Emma Peel. She told *TV Times*, "I did it because I had left the Royal Shakespeare Company knowing that if I renewed my contract and stayed on for three or four years, I would have progressed and played good parts, but I was yearning for additional scope. To accomplish this I would have to plunge into the deep end, and nothing seemed deeper than this. I was right. Nothing is deeper."

Which was not to say she in any way severed her relationship with the RSC; after her first season of *The Avengers* she returned to Stratford to appear as Viola in *Twelfth Night*. By that time, frazzled by the exhausting production schedule and overwhelmed by the attention Peel was garnering from fans and critics, Rigg had told producers she didn't think she would return for the next season, the first to be shot in color specifically for its U.S. telecast. However, the producers weren't easily put off. Rigg recalled to *Oui*, "I was pursued by my producers who said, 'Come back and do another forty episodes,' and I liked the idea of doing both Viola and Emma Peel at the same time." Producers adjusted the shooting schedule so Rigg could continue as Viola while the series was in production.

So, she returned to the series and once again found herself in the all-consuming repetition of producing an hour episodic. A telephone service would ring with a 6:30 A.M. wake-up call. "I'm never late," she told *TV Times*, "comatose that I still am, and I hate that sound of the bell—at this ghastly hour. I've got no vanity at that time of the morning." It would take Rigg twenty minutes to bathe and suck down a glass of lemon juice and then she would be picked up by her studio chauffeur, John Taylor, who also ran errands for Diana, including grocery shopping, while she was on the set. "I wouldn't know what to do without him," she said more than once.

Diana was also close to her stand-in, Diana Enright, and her look-alike stunt double, Cyd Child. While Rigg indeed had been taught how to flip an assailant over her head, she wasn't exactly the Jackie Chan of the sixties, so Child's work was extremely important to the look and action of the show. Ironically, Child bore such a striking resemblance to Diana that more than once she was filmed with her face toward the camera, and according to a variety of *Avengers* resources, fans never once complained.

Choreographing the fight sequences was coordinator Ray Austin, who has since gone on to be a highly regarded television director in Hollywood. Austin, who began as a stuntman and also did bit acting parts while working as Cary Grant's driver part time, is believed to be the first to present a karate fight on broadcast television, despite concerns by studio lawyers that British schoolchildren would copy Rigg's moves and use them against other children during school-yard fights.

When she was safely tucked away at the studio filming, Rigg was blissfully oblivious to *The Avengers* phenomenon. But out in public, the attention she generated left her unsettled and feeling immensely vulnerable. "It was frightening," she admitted. "I was used to strolling in the street without a second thought. And suddenly everyone was looking at you wherever you went, nudging, winking." The carnal interest in her exhibited by strangers made Diana revert emotionally back to adolescence. "I was a kind of good middle-class English girl who'd gone to a Moravian school," she told the *Sun Herald* in 2002. "Moravians are akin to Quakers and in the old days—I don't think they do anymore—they'd bury the man on one side and the women on the other and never the twain shall mix. Even in death. So I was quite properly brought up and then suddenly there's this in-your-face lust coming from all sides and I just found it very . . . I think if it had happened now, I mean, I'm not saying at my age, but if I was sort of that age and it was happening now I'd be able to cope with it because sex is everywhere. Sex is on the television, books, magazines. But then it wasn't, so it was quite discomfiting. I should have been flattered but I wasn't." Looking back, Rigg admits that she simply didn't understand other people's attraction to her at the time: "Sometimes I see photographs of myself and think, God, I really *was* quite tasty. But I didn't know it at the time."

Rigg believes her height sometimes caught people off guard. "I always think of myself as a tall, large person, because, I suppose, as an adolescent my height was the one thing that I wanted really to change more than anything else," she told *Cosmopolitan* in 1976. "I found being tall a terrible hang-up. I was always noticed, always the one caught doing anything evil, whereas my small, blond friends always got away with things. So I think that's the main impression I make on people, and also the most surprising because they imagine me much smaller. They have seen me on a tiny screen in their living rooms, so they think I'm tiny."

When she traveled, Rigg would deny her identity to any fan bold enough to approach her. "It was not easy to say I was not Mrs. Peel," Diana Rigg admitted to Henry Gris, "because I dislike lies. But I would have had to explain why and what I was doing there, and it was a long story." But denials didn't always work. She once had to barricade herself in the bathroom after a group of fans spotted her at a motor show and started a stampede in her direction.

"I had become paranoid," she observed to the *Sunday Telegraph*, "with an underlying urge to pack and run. It is a curious thing. People who have never been subjected to it can never really understand what it means. I can only describe it as a sense of panic that seizes you when you are Diana to yourself and you are walking down the street. An instant later, you are somebody else to a lot of people who behave as if you belong to them. If you are quite a private person, which I am, this seems an intrusion on my privacy. I just have to run."

As the show's popularity increased internationally, the fan mail kept arriving in ever greater numbers and caused Diana much angst. She explained her moral dilemma to *TV Times*: "I am supposed to answer them. But I can't, and that worries me deeply. I get persecuted by the mere thought that there's an obligation which I am not willing to fulfill." She turned to her mother for help, appointing her to manage the torrent of fan mail from their family home in Leeds. "We have this room at home, measuring twenty feet by fifteen feet, and it is full of letters," she explained. "More are delivered each day—all addressed to me. That is where mother comes in. She reads, and she answers. And I feel ashamed. But I can't help it."

Rigg quickly learned the same sobering truth any modern celebrity is confronted with: while most fan letters are just notes of encouragement or thanks from appreciative fans who enjoy the actor's talent and screen presence, there is a percentage of people who become inappropriately and, in some cases, disturbingly attached. "People have made up their minds to identify me with a fantasy of theirs on television. In their minds they want to have a relationship with me based on fantasy which can take any form. I have heard from my mother that there have been letters from children saying, 'You look like my dead mother and so I write to you.' I think that is terrifying."

Less terrifying and more typical were lustful letters from hormone-driven teenagers expressing their attraction for Diana/Emma. Beryl Rigg would send a response more abrupt than a cold shower. Diana explained, "My mum was

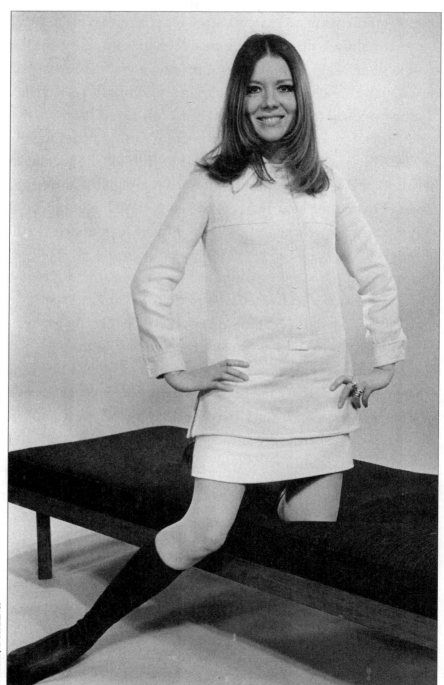

wonderful. I just used to pass over this pile of envelopes to her and she'd open all these letters from lovesick youths and she used to say things like, 'Those aren't very nice thoughts, and besides, my daughter's too old for you. What you need is a good run around the block.'"

Years later, Rigg would reflect on those days and regret she hadn't been able to relax more. "I should have handled it better, had more fun," she admitted to the *Sunday Telegraph Magazine*. "Not naughty fun. But just, you know . . . I sometimes think when I look back on those days, '*Why didn't I have more confidence? Why didn't I know I was pretty good-looking?*' It is probably to do with my Yorkshire upbringing. Always thinking that people might be saying, 'Who does she think she is?'"

However, her worry about niceties was quickly forgotten when she discovered she was getting paid less on *The Avengers* than the cameraman. Her reaction was immediate and decisive. "Outrage!" she recounted to the *Sun Herald*. "I kicked up a fuss and I became incredibly unpopular as a result because the English press absolutely latched on to it and I was made out to be mercenary and a jumped-up actress who should be grateful for her opportunity." Rigg told David Nathan they missed the point. "At the time, it was considered very bad form to suggest that you were not getting enough. I did not feel that I was worth more because I was successful on television but because Patrick and I were carrying a highly successful series and I was getting ninety pounds a week while the cameraman was pulling in £120.

"The fact is that my agent at the time had not equipped

himself with enough knowledge to bargain properly for a decent price for me. No, I didn't stamp my foot. All I said was, 'Look, this is unfair,' and I got double, £180. It still wasn't a huge amount. Any argument about money is ugly, but at the same time I felt I was being exploited and I had to put a stop to it. Even now, although it is being shown all over the world, I'm lucky if I get an occasional cheque for some paltry sum."

The issue of payment would linger for many years to come. In 1973, Rigg commented during a *Los Angeles* magazine profile that she had never really received proper residuals from all the international success of *The Avengers*. "Of course it *would* be nice if there were money filtering into the bank from that," she said. "Would that one had some residuals from all that, one would be quite rich, but Patrick Macnee and I would have to get organized, and be completely mercenary, and have a lawsuit or something, and I'm not about to do that. What's done is done. I love working and make a good living."

Even though the producers had agreed to increase her salary, Rigg later admitted the only reason she didn't bolt right then was out of loyalty to Macnee, who she affectionately referred to as Paddy Nee. "I am devoted to Patrick," she says. "I'm frightened of minimizing him by talking about him, because it always sounds so glib, but he's an extremely generous and gentle and marvelous man."

But Rigg also craved new opportunities and challenges more than she did the steady income of a successful television series, so she made it clear that the following season would be her last. She explains, "I wasn't thinking anymore as Emma Peel. I was simply learning lines and that's not good enough.

I think one ought to develop and that's why I left. One of the attractions that make this business so exciting and wonderful is realizing new characters. Mind you, I am not ungrateful. I will be the last to minimize what television has done for me. It is a phenomenon, a miracle medium that can accomplish in six months what takes years on the stage. Suddenly, you are famous. Suddenly, everybody knows you. The point is, though, that you are not yourself. Only the other person you portray in the series. That person is, of necessity, imposed by television, one-dimensional. You ask yourself, is it worth it?" On a less thoughtful note, she said, "If I have to toss one more villain over my shoulder I think I'll scream."

When weighing the situation objectively, there was only one honest resolution for Rigg. "I simply had to leave the series," she said. "*The Avengers* was fun, but I had no idea when I followed Honor that it would make me a name like this. I began to feel claustrophobic. I began to feel *The Avengers* was taking over. The degree of success it was getting made it more and more difficult to leave as the weeks went by. If I had stayed, I would have been under pressure by forces outside myself. I knew I had to go, and why wait till I was stale if I could leave on a high note?" On a side note, the kind of control studios and networks tried to exert was annoying as well. She revealed to *TV Guide,* "The studio never liked me to give interviews. I would always try to speak the truth, you see. You've got to be honest in this business. The public believes in you."

Whether it was simply a casting stunt or that producers were hopeful of luring her back to reprise the role of

Cathy Gale, they offered Honor Blackman a guest spot. But she brusquely rejected the overture, telling the *Daily Mail*, "There's nothing new to get out of it—I want to go forward, not backward."

Rigg understood the sentiment and was looking forward to life after *The Avengers*. But she never could have dreamed how inextricably entwined her entire career would be with the series or how Emma Peel would become her signature role for fans of the next several generations. But more than that, Emma Peel has become an archetype for how a television character can embody social change even before the citizenry is aware the change is occurring.

In 1998, Maria Alvarez wrote an opinion piece in the *New Statesman*: "For me, and for a host of women who grew up on the original sixties *Avengers*, Emma Peel represented our first thoroughly British feminist fantasy figure. Beside her, the contemporary airhead ladies and all those current avatars of girl power who grace the cover of *FHM* and *Loaded* are fluffy companions for a regressive new lad: and as unthreatening as a Spam sandwich.

"It was only the sci-fi, surreally comic genre of *The Avengers* that prevented most men from glimpsing the terrible truth: that the enigmatic, leather-clad Mrs. Peel was a femme fatale of the Pop Art order. The Peel appeal lay in her maturity, in the combination of athleticism, ruthlessness and cool intellect which had her dispensing verbal and physical karate chops without so much as a flinch of guilt. She was the Bond girl with a first-class brain and a 24-carat steely blitheness.

"In her Diana Rigg incarnation, Mrs. Peel was post-feminist (in the sense that she took feminism for granted) before her time: in one episode, coming across the villainess tied to a pillar, she asks her with that trademark ironical smile, 'Didn't we get the vote?' . . .

"This mixture of feline and phallic, of danger and eroticism, seemed as integral to her style and personality as the smooth leather and kinky boots that encased her were testaments to self-containment and enigma. She was sleekness and movement personified: the archetypal modern action woman."

As Robin Dougherty observed on Salon.com in 1999, "Not only had Rigg's character broken all the rules that said good girls don't hit their attackers, she also exercised a bold new sexual and social freedom, living alone and quite independently. ('It was a case of life imitating art,' Rigg once said. 'I was like that myself to a degree.') . . . Rigg was a well-fitted foil for Macnee's Steed, whose old-world charm (he was something of a Regency dandy) superbly complemented Emma's mod fashions and sporty '60s lifestyle. Their characters coasted on style as much as their crime-fighting finesse, and Rigg's Emma became an icon of cool. Unlike practically every other babe on big screens and little, Emma was her partner's professional equal and not a toy. . . .

"Despite her short stay on *The Avengers*, Rigg's arrival had signaled a startling new kind of TV heroine. Her trademark karate poses, stylized as they seem now, made her the rare woman who approached the world with a physicality that wasn't entirely based on her sex appeal. She could fight back."

Rigg was aware even while she was doing *The Avengers* that more positives would come from the role than negatives. "Emma Peel did a lot for me besides making me well-known over most of the world," she observed. "I used to be shy about myself. I was worried about the avalanche of fan mail. The Royal Shakespeare Company doesn't prepare you for that. But I've come to realize and appreciate the interest viewers have in television people. It's surprising—and touching—that nearly a year later so many should write that they regret my departure." Time would give her even greater perspective. In 1995, she said with some surprise, "Middle-aged women still approach me to talk about Peel. For the first time they realized women could change things without men's help." And in *The Avengers Companion*, Rigg is quoted as saying: "Emma Peel was definitely a different type of character for television. For the first time a woman in a TV series was intelligent, independent and capable of looking after herself. That is why the show became such a success—it reflected what was happening to women throughout the world in the '60s."

Responding to a comment by feminist writer Susan Brownmiller that Peel was nothing short of heroic, Rigg would say in 1999 to Vince Cosgrove, "She's probably right. . . . Emma was uncompromisingly her own person, and she was clever; she could look after herself but she wasn't a feminist in the strident sense of the word. Yes, she was an icon—and will remain so."

And indeed it continues to resonate with new generations who find the show. Rigg explained, "I still get letters from some very odd people. It's curious. Apart from the fellows—

or the women—who obviously dig the foot-fetishism part of it or the black leather or the whipping, I get letters from professors and university students who just say how much they loved it and I consider it a much more literate series than anything they get handed out. Therefore they think of me as an intelligent person."

While some actors closely associated with particular roles—think Adam West and *Batman*—blame the character for career stagnation, Diana is refreshingly resistant to that crutch. In an interview with Michael Leech, she admitted, "It was indeed a great change to jump into all that black leather and boots after feathery dresses and those Shakespeare ladies. I thoroughly enjoyed it. I'm still amazed that one television series can make one's name so well-known. You transfer from all that hard work onstage and do a few days in front of a camera—and suddenly your name is a household word."

She told John Koch of the *Boston Globe* that portraying Emma Peel, "never stopped me from doing anything, I don't think." She continued, saying, "The only area in which I've not been able to do anything I'm proud of is film. Perhaps that happened because I was a television star. There's a sort of reluctance to employ television stars in films. And it's quite interesting, because many, many years later, I think this still ever so slightly prevails. . . . Although I very seldom watch myself, I did see [*Hospital*] recently, and I felt, ugh, I could have done so much better."

Although many of her theater compatriots might have thought it blasphemous, Diana said she learned some invaluable acting lessons during her tenure on the series: "Television taught me an economy of style I didn't have before. I feel it has done me nothing but good. When I meet directors now my attitude is different. I can be constructive instead of simply being an instrument of theirs. However, I still very firmly believe that being in theater and working away is the very best way to learn your craft."

As it became clear to the producers that Rigg was not going to capitulate and change her mind at the last minute, they were once again faced with the problem of how to write the female lead off the show. Many fans worried the producers would kill Peel out of spite, but in the end, her farewell was tender, if a bit anticlimactic. According to a Web site on the show (www.theavengers.tv), Rigg's last appearance as Peel occurred months after she had left the show. Producers had hired actress Linda Thorson to play the role of Steed's new sidekick, Tara King, and were filming her third episode called "The Forget-Me-Knot." Because of some clause in her contract, Rigg was required to come back for four days' work, and in the episode, she temporarily loses her memory after being administered some amnesia-inducing drug. At the end, it's revealed that Mrs. Peel's long lost husband, Peter, has found his way out of the Amazonian jungle. Rather hilariously, when he shows up, he's dressed just like Steed. But the scene turns emotional as Emma says good-bye to John. According to the site, the scene was so emotional that Macnee sat crying in his dressing room afterward.

Although some fans have blamed Rigg's departure as being the death knell for *The Avengers*, the series was simply a victim of the cold realities of television economics. Because the producers had become reliant on the license fee paid by ABC in the U.S., the series' survival depended on its continued success in America. However, the year of the Tara King season, *The Avengers* was scheduled opposite a new show debuting on NBC called *Laugh-In*, which was destined to become a huge pop-culture hit in its own right. Without Rigg as a draw, *Laugh-In* demolished *The Avengers* in the ratings, and ABC chose not to renew its option for the 1969-1970 television season. When news of the cancellation reached the producers in London, *The Avengers* abruptly stopped production in February 1969, ending one of the most successful runs in British television history.

Chapter Seven

• • • •

W H I L E fans lamented her departure from *The Avengers*, Rigg was getting on with her life. She and her longtime paramour Philip Saville had moved out of her old mews cottage and into a home that was once artist Augustus John's studio, and reveled in their bohemian existence. Reminiscing years later to the *Sunday Times* about those days, Rigg noted, "It was terrific in a way. It was very good for my generation. We had had all these awful middle-aged constraints put on us for years, and suddenly it was us, we were at the forefront, we were leading. We got credence from the success of all these young writers and musicians. But at the same time there was a lot of rubbish going on on the sidelines. All that flower talk." Rigg said dismissively, "I couldn't *man* anybody."

Instead, Rigg and Saville shared a home as partners, even though Saville was still married to his wife. It was a situation Rigg systematically dismissed: "It is probably easier to categorize one as married, just about to be or having been but I won't subscribe to categorization." The more her notoriety and recognizability increased during her tenure on *The Avengers*, the more she jealously guarded her privacy. Although she still loved going out, having a house brought out Diana's domestic side. She discovered a latent passion for cooking and often invited friends over for dinner, which she prepared in her brand-new, $8,000 all-electric kitchen using home-grown herbs, which she grew in window boxes outside her kitchen. Rigg had a virtual herb farm, harvesting sage, thyme, marjoram, rosemary, chervil, two kinds of mint, sorrel and bay trees which she enthused "are marvelous for fish."

In an interview with *TV Times*, Diana explained that having her own house allowed her to fulfill some less-than-theatrical dreams. "I had always wanted to grow my own herbs," she said. "This was my obsession. So I got the address of an herb farm ninety-five miles out of town, and one morning I went there. A little old lady took me around and she muttered under her breath and said they would never grow in the London smoke. I said I'd like to try anyway. So, she shook her head and gave me what I wanted.

"They came in little pots, as I brought them back to London they were all looking sad and sick. So I put them in larger pots and stuck them in my window boxes and every day I watered them out of a jug. And the miracle came to pass."

While working on the television series, Rigg had taken driving lessons and gotten her license. She learned to drive in the spring, so when winter arrived, she found herself struggling with the challenges of controlling a car on icy roads. She told Henry Gris about the time she flew to Switzerland for a quick getaway weekend at the Klosters ski resort: "I drove through the night, with the craziest Swiss drivers whizzing past me over the ice-covered road. It twisted its way through the mountains, and I just hung on the wheel and prayed. I could have turned back, but I didn't—too proud."

Of course, some of Rigg's theater cohorts might have taken issue with that self-assessment. Peter Hall once came to Diana's defense. "It is all very well to sneer at popular television success," he said, "but what *The Avengers* and stardom gave Diana was a kind of centered confidence that she didn't have as a young girl." Thus, she was confident, not proud.

Now having the benefit of some time and distance from the initial rush of disapproval, Rigg could look at the bigger picture. "They thought I was profligate with my talent," she mused. "But fair is fair: they had also invested three years training me within the company, so I suppose they saw it as a waste. Yes, at the time it smacked of perversity, but it turned out to be safe. Emma Peel never did me any harm. In fact she has done me nothing but good. It wasn't harmful. How could it be? It catapulted me to the kind of fame that would have taken twenty years solid touring to achieve."

While earning the label "TV star" might not have been harmful, there were some drawbacks that became apparent, most notably the lack of interest from feature-film producers to hire her for high-profile roles. "I kept being offered gun-toting parts and I didn't really want that," she admitted to *Theater Week*. "Most of the plum movie roles went instead to Vanessa Redgrave or Glenda Jackson. I came a very poor third." This was true not only in Britain; most Hollywood studios seemed equally disinterested. "There were some offers, but not many," she explained. "There has always been a certain reticence in Hollywood to employ people who have been television stars, perhaps because they come with so much baggage." Maybe so, but Rigg was offered $200,000 to appear in a Hollywood film and turned it down because the role disinterested her. As she put it, "So far I have not been offered anything I want. I don't want a long-term contract. As an actress I will work where and for whom I want, if the script is exciting enough. If a script is good and they have a director I can trust, then I will do it."

However, Rigg's fuse was short when she saw any intimation she was being typecast. She recounted to *TV Times* that she once met a director at a party who wooed her with a script he promised was perfect for her. Intrigued, Diana asked him to send her a copy. "Well, if I wasn't the girl who comes tearing through the door with a gun in one hand and a flamethrower in the other, I was the sexy siren sneaking through the door in Veronica Lake style," she said. "I lost my temper, for the first time. I sent them a message saying that I couldn't do it." In a calmer moment, she allowed, "It's not absolutely deliberate. When I finished *The Avengers* I was offered—in those days the span of parts for women was terribly limited—and I was just offered these, you know, gun-toting women and I thought, God in Heaven, I hadn't left *The Avengers* just to do that on a bigger screen, so I said no."

Well, maybe not all the time. On an *Avengers* Web site (www.theavengers.tv), the odd caper of Diana Rigg's career after *The Avengers* is revealed: the silent short films *Das Diadem* and *The Mini-Killers*. Apparently, however, this is a mystery that not even John Steed could solve. Both films were shot on eight-millimeter film, meaning they are the quality of pre-digital home movies, and you will not find them listed on any official Rigg filmography. From the descriptions given, the films almost sound like outtakes or a presentation or perhaps even screen tests. Both films—which are copyrighted to Accentfilm in Dusseldorf, Germany—have been distributed to fans via a French Web site called Friends of Steed.

Made in 1966, *Das Diadem* was available in two forms—a nineteen-minute silent version and a twelve-minute version with sound. According to the site, the longer version may have been a work print, the shorter film the final edited-down version. A source is quoted as saying of the longer version, ". . . the extra scenes on it are the sort of scenes which would be removed. At one point, while chasing the baddie at the pool there is a close-up of Rigg's face showing various expressions that seems to go on forever. Also, the scene where she is swimming with the dolphins is painfully long!"

The Mini-Killers is believed to have been made shortly after Diana left *The Avengers*. It consisted of four parts: *Operation Costa Brava, Heroin, Macabre* and *Flamenco*. In addition to starring Rigg it featured Jose Nieto, Jack Rocha, H. Coscollin, Madame Million and El Sali. According to the Web site: "A press piece from 1969 (from an unknown magazine, which could possibly be *Photoplay*) has a shot of Diana Rigg from part three of *The Mini-Killers* and, after explaining that she has just been seen in *The Assassination Bureau* and is about to be seen in *On Her Majesty's Secret Service*, says 'Obviously, the "quiet" life was not to her taste, for she went to Spain to star in *The Mini-Killers*, another all-action, fast-moving thriller.' There are some interesting implications from this piece—*The Mini-Killers* was obviously seen as a 'proper' film by the magazine; the existence of a promotional photo implies that it was being marketed as such; something must have gone very wrong." The copies of this film that survive again have no sound and so far, nobody has come forward with an explanation of how either *Das Diadem* or *The Mini-Killers* came into being or how Rigg became involved in the projects.

What is clear is that once she finished with *The Avengers*, Rigg needed to return to her thespian womb. And despite the snide comments she got when agreeing to do the series, it seems that her increased profile may have helped her be cast as one of the leads in the Royal Shakespeare Company's 1968 film production of *A Midsummer Night's Dream*, which also featured Helen Mirren, Ian Richardson and Judi Dench. Rigg said that her decision to maintain her close ties with theater rather than try to capitalize on *The Avengers* by taking any film offer that came her way was in part inspired by Paul Scofield, who won the Best Actor Oscar for the 1966 film *A Man for All Seasons*. Diana had appeared with Scofield when she toured with *King Lear* prior to being cast as Emma Peel. "He's been my ideal since I first saw him on the stage," she explained. "I was working with him in *King Lear* when I became aware of his sense of identity, a strong, totally compromising identity. The beauty of it is that here is a man who has just won an Oscar in an Oscar-winning film and Hollywood is after him. What does he do? He's gone back to Stratford. Obviously, he doesn't care for the money. And he's right. Of course, it's your beliefs that matter. In a way I followed his example when I agreed to film *A Midsummer Night's Dream*. Peter Brook was doing it and I believe in him and I grew up with him, so I had to answer his call. Professionally speaking, I am part of his troupe—even though I think I'm too bad for the part." For Rigg, it was all about the work; the money would follow. "Money is so transitory. I will not forget that I could, when forced to, live on seven pounds a week," she remarked.

It's a good thing Rigg wasn't a diva because by Hollywood standards, the actors who worked on *A Midsummer Night's Dream* were roughing it. Whereas major studios transport their stars back and forth from the sound stage or location in limos or chauffeured town cars and supply talent with comfortable trailers, Brooks' production was a bit of an endurance test. "There was a great deal of discomfort," Diana told the *San Francisco Examiner and Chronicle* in late 1967. "Nobody got star treatment. Nobody had stand-ins. We did our own standing in." She would later add to *TV Guide*, "I did my own makeup, for what it's worth, since I'm covered with mud most of the time. But I had to look sixteen and that was more difficult." However, she also told the *Examiner and Chronicle*, "For me it represented everything a film should be, working with actors and actresses who I admired and respected."

Rigg also argued that creature comforts meant nothing if actors were excluded from being active participants in the creative process of moviemaking—a typical scenario in big-budget Hollywood fare. She explained: "Basically they give you what they consider the star treatment and at the same time exclude you from the very important part of film-ing—the talking, discussing and working out things with the director, almost on an improvisation level. I don't want to be excluded. More often they treat you with the deep sus-picion that you're going to turn difficult. If people do turn difficult, they generally do because they are misunderstood, not treated as a human being. Also, a great deal of money is wasted, and where there is a great deal of money there is a great deal of panic. This is what I detest, the basic insecurity of these people who don't have their own standards, their own attitudes. Everything is based on the person directly above them."

That said, however, a month later Rigg began production on Paramount Pictures' *The Assassination Bureau*, which was released in 1969. The plot of the film, a farcical action-adven-ture romp set in pre-World War I Victorian London, centered around a female reporter who investigates a society of inter-national assassins who kill people that are deemed to deserve it—all for a price, of course. The film is based on an unfin-ished novel by Jack London, who died in 1916. Supposedly, London bought the plot idea from a young Sinclair Lewis but abandoned the project in 1910 after writing 101 pages. Almost half a century later, historian Robert L. Fish discovered the manuscript and wrote the last fifty-one pages, publishing it in 1963. The film costarred Oliver Reed and Telly Savalas, and Rigg called it "the best film script I [had] read for a long time." She explained, "Basically it is the turn of the century when all those archdukes and kings were being assassinated and I, as a journalist, attempt to uncover the assassination

Rigg after a scene from her film *The Assassination Bureau*

bureau with some astonishing results. The point is, it's at a time when there were no female journalists so she is a militant feminist."

However, reactions to the film were mixed, both when it was released and now in its afterlife on home video and DVD. Reviewer Graeme Clark said, "It's all rather arch, rather contrived, and has a touch of nastiness to give it an edge. While Rigg and Reed get by on their natural charm, everyone else is simply playing a caricature; the Bureau themselves don't really convince as expert killers—only Savalas is a genuine threat. It has its moments, like the grand finale on a zeppelin which carries a huge bomb, but it could have been funnier. And the special effects are fairly cheap looking—all the money must have gone on the sets and costumes."

The review on Epinions.com reflects the breezy character of the film: "Diana Rigg is an enchanting 31 years old in this movie, fresh from her success as Emma Peel in *The Avengers*. She is more demure and ladylike in this film, but shows amazing courage and ingenuity. She is fighting for women's rights, and for her right to be a newspaper reporter, while the menfolk indulgently dismiss her as being a little peculiar.

"Oliver Reed is, well, Oliver Reed. Dashing, handsome, athletic, always there to rescue the fair maiden, when she was not rescuing him.

"Telly Savalas was er . . . different. Can you imagine him with a slight British accent, and oh so perfect manners? Not quite the rough and tumble detective Kojak I was used to, but he played his part to perfection.

"This is a swashbuckling British film that really swashbuckles."

Rigg found the experience of moviemaking a technical challenge compared to acting for the stage. She noted, "In a play you learn the blocking and you don't have to worry so much about moving to specific points. You sort of take it for granted. In film you're always conscious of your physical movement because you have to be within the camera's range. Of course you can never look at the camera so you always have to move to marks, without looking at down."

Had it not been for a family crisis, Rigg's next role may have very well been the female lead in the film version of a musical. Diana told Robert Musel of *TV Guide*, "Alan Jay Lerner, who wrote *My Fair Lady*, came over to ask me to play in the film version of his musical, *Paint Your Wagon*. I sang him an ancient lullaby and he thought that with a few singing lessons I could do it. The part calls for a Southern girl, and Joshua Logan, who is directing, thought I could pick that up in a few lessons, too. But my father is very ill and I could not possibly leave." Instead, Rigg planned to take some time off to be near her parents. "It will give me time to think," she said. "Three or four months of concentration and some sort of privacy will be good for me. All my life I've been precipitated into everything—modeling, the stage, even *The Avengers*."

Fans of the swingin' Emma Peel may have been surprised to learn that off-camera Rigg found solace and strength in religion. "I don't accept all the tenets of the Christian ethic, not one hundred percent," Diana qualifies. "Very curiously, morality says you shouldn't live together outside the state of wedlock. And I say, until you are prepared to make the vows

Rigg in *The Assassination Bureau*

and stick by them, then that's the only thing to do. But belief is very important in my life. I'm slightly old-fashioned; love a sermon, love our hymns." She told Pauline Peters that, as opposed to praying, "I have a conversation." She went on, "I find that the answers are delayed until the following Sunday in church. I always get an answer somewhere along the line. Not a voice. But always during the service something strikes a chord and I think, '*Oh, that's the way to look at it.*' And as I careened through late adolescence and my twenties and thirties it was always there."

In the late 1960s Rigg seemed content to nurture her aesthetic soul through her work with the Royal Shakespeare Company while padding her bank account with film roles. And while *The Assassination Bureau* might have been destined to be a largely forgotten bit of cinematic fluff, her next film would once again find Diana making pop-culture history.

Chapter Eight

• • • •

THERE has simply not been a more enduring, success-ful film franchise than the twenty-one James Bond movies. Spanning four decades, the films have gener-ated over $3.3 billion dollars in box-office revenue—and that's not including video sales and licensing income. Even though the five *Star Wars* films have inched past, earning $3.4 billion, when adjusted for inflation 007 still reigns supreme.

When Diana Rigg was cast to be the female lead in *On Her Majesty's Secret Service*, the franchise was at a turning point. Sean Connery, who had brought the suave Cold War spy to cinematic life with an appealing combination of self-deprecating humor, derring-do and impeccable manners that softened his lusty appreciation for beautiful women, had left the franchise after doing five films in six years amid bitter rancor. He had grown to hate his embodiment of Bond—and the typecasting that came with it. But the character was so popular, producers felt confident the franchise could survive Connery's departure.

That hadn't always been the case. Bond was the creation of Ian Fleming, a former naval intelligence officer. After leaving the military Fleming worked for a while as a journalist, then retreated to his Jamaican estate, Goldeneye, where he wrote his first novel, *Casino Royale,* which introduced a suave, champagne-loving British Secret Service agent named James Bond. Instead of thinking up the name himself, Fleming simply used the name of real-life author and ornithologist James Bond, who had written *The Ultimate Guide Book to Birds in the West Indies*, a coffee table book his wife happened to be reading at the time. Pictures and interviews with Fleming leave the distinct impression there was more than a little Walter Mitty-esque vicarious living involved with creating Bond, who had impeccable taste, impeccable manners and whom women found irresistible.

However, readers found *Casino Royale* easily resistible. The novel did so poorly in its hardback edition that the publisher released the paperback with a new title: *You Asked for It.* They promoted the new title with a suggestive cover featuring a scantily clad woman looking as if she's about to have an erotic encounter with the man in the background pouring himself a drink. Unfortunately, this failed to generate any interest in the book. Undaunted, Fleming continued to write about the super spy and eventually his books began to gain a following—with the help of President John Kennedy, whose comment about liking the Bond novel spurred a sales spike for the books. Fleming wrote a total of fourteen Bond books before dying suddenly of a heart attack in 1964, when he was only fifty-six years old. He died during the filming of *Goldfin-*

ger, which starred former *Avengers* star Honor Blackman as Pussy Galore.

The first novel turned into a movie was *Dr. No* in 1962, featuring Ursula Andress as the first "Bond Girl," Honey Rider, who made her unforgettable entrance by walking out of the ocean in a bikini—and holding a knife. Although the early Bond Girls were imbued with a certain pluckiness, the fact that these characters mostly swooned at Bond's feet (and their physical appearances seemed more important than their acting skills) created the perception that the actresses themselves were little more than eye candy. Despite the high-profile nature of the roles, and the big box office the movies generated, few Bond Girls moved on to bigger and better things. Thus the Bond Curse was born.

In the AMC documentary *Bond Girls Are Forever*, written and produced by former Bond Girl Maryam D'Abo, Italian actress Luciana Paluzzi complained that after appearing in 1965's *Thunderball* as villainess Fiona Volpi, she was shocked that her credibility as an actress had been compromised. "To do a Bond picture is a blessing, but it's also a curse," she said. "Because when I went back to Italy . . . the Fellinis, Antonionis and Viscontis of the time, they didn't want to have anything to do with me. . . . They were all very nice, but when it came to one of their pictures—no."

Says D'Abo: "The film industry didn't want to use her because she'd been in this action movie. In the sixties it was so new and like a comic strip."

Model-turned-actress Maud Adams, who appeared in *The Man With the Golden Gun* and *Octopussy* told Sharon Swart,

"At the time, the Bond films were quite different from today. Women were generally portrayed as damsels in distress. As an actress it's not really the most wonderful part to play, but I was also fairly new to the profession and I knew that this was a very decorative part."

But being a Bond Girl could also be lucrative, especially for a theater actress. Rigg says she was "paid zonking amounts" and was taken to Paris for dress fittings as an added perk. But her big pay day would come with some big headaches, courtesy of her costar, George Lazenby.

After Sean Connery turned in his license to kill, producers Albert "Cubby" Broccoli and Harry Saltzman conducted what United Artist claimed was the "biggest star search in film history." Somewhat curiously, out of the four hundred actors who auditioned, the producers hired an unknown twenty-nine-year-old Australian model named George Lazenby to star in the next Bond feature, *On Her Majesty's Secret Service*. More curious is that the man they expected to carry the studio's successful film franchise had never acted before, nor was he acquainted with the ways of Hollywood. It would show almost immediately.

Lazenby was born on September 5, 1939, in Goulburn, Australia, a small town of 30,000 people located about two hours west of Sydney. George was athletic as a child and enjoyed any and all outdoor activities, from swimming to hunting. When he was just fourteen, his father got him a job on the railroad. After two years, George joined the Australian army and ended up in Special Forces, where he was trained in martial arts, earning a black belt. Lazenby spent five years in the military and once he was discharged, he settled in Canberra where he was hired as an apprentice car mechanic. Two years later, he was promoted to car salesman. When a girl he was dating moved to England, he decided to follow her there and in 1964 bought a one-way ticket to London. However, his visions of a romantic reunion were quickly doused. "I thought it would be great to be with her again but when I got there, she wouldn't even talk to me," he recalled. Bitter, with just $800 in his pocket and no real plan, he rented a room in Earls Court, London, which he says "was so small you had to dress in the corridor."

He found work as a Mercedes car salesman and it was while he was at work one day in the car showroom that a freelance photographer named Chard Jenkins suggested he would make a good model. Willing to give it a try, George got a portfolio together and by 1965 was earning enough money that he quit his salesman job. By the following year he was one of the top models in England. Perhaps his highest-profile job was as the Big Fry Guy in the Big Fry Chocolate Bar commercials in London. Lazenby was making a six-figure income and living a lavish lifestyle that would almost rival that of James Bond.

George was working in Paris when he found out he was to audition for James Bond. Over the years, Cubby Broccoli has told a story about how he once met Lazenby in a barber shop and thought then he would make a good Bond. Lazenby told *Movie Collector* it didn't quite happen that way: "Well, that was untrue. That came about because I went to the barber to get my hair cut like Sean Connery to go down to my first interview with Cubby Broccoli, and he happened to be in there at the time. The barber pointed out to him later on, 'Remember that guy who got the James Bond thing? He was in here at the same time you were.' I just wanted to get a haircut like Connery's and I knew where Connery got his hair cut."

Although after his test the producers expressed some reservations over his lack of experience, director Peter Hunt wholeheartedly supported Lazenby. Much of the appeal was his physical presence; at 6'2" and 186 pounds, Lazenby looked the part. Plus, he was a skilled scuba diver and skier and had been trained in self-defense during his stint in the Australian army. Figuring he would grow into the role, the producers signed Lazenby to a $50,000 contract. He would later recall, "I had no acting experience, I was coming from the male model point of view. I walked in looking like James Bond, and acting as if that's the way I was anyway. And they thought, *'All we have to do is keep this guy just the way he is and we'll have James Bond.'*"

George fancied that his personality was also suited to play a character like James Bond. "I am very much a loner. I like it that way," he says. "Besides, traveling around so much as a model meant that I found myself with suitcases and acquaintances in London, Paris, Rome, New York, Zurich, Monte Carlo and so on, but a very few firm friends anywhere." Unfortunately, being cast as James Bond wouldn't make him many friends, either.

Like Lazenby, Rigg had beat out some big-name film actresses, including Brigitte Bardot and Catherine Deneuve, to win the pivotal role of Tracy. One reason there was such interest is that *On Her Majesty's Secret Service* was the only Fleming novel in which James Bond falls in love and gets married. In early production meetings, Saltzman wanted a blonde actress, in keeping with the characters as portrayed in the novel. In 1995, Peter Hunt recalled how the producer set his sights on Brigitte Bardot: "She was one of the choices. Harry was very keen on her playing the part and went to France to meet with her. I met with her on three occasions. We had lunch and we had drinks in the evening. But on the third visit she just calmly announced that she had just signed a deal to do *Shalako*—with Sean Connery! So Harry and I looked at one another and that was the end of that."

Saltzman then began to pursue Catherine Deneuve. "I didn't actually meet with her," said Hunt, "but she was discussed. I'm not sure she wanted to do it actually. Harry tried to contact her and get her but I don't think she was keen on the idea." Nor did Hunt seem particularly keen on either of Saltzman's suggestions. But when Diana Rigg's name came up, Hunt knew immediately she was the ideal Tracy. He explained, "At the time we got Diana Rigg we were still talking about George Lazenby and my point was that if we were going to have somebody like George Lazenby, who was really not an actor and hadn't done that much, I insisted on having a really good actress. I wanted somebody really excellent and, of course, she jumped to mind. Her agent, Dennis Selinger, was around doing other things and when we broached it to him he jumped at it and said, 'Well, let me talk to her,' and when I got her, when she said she would do it, there was no doubt in my mind that we would have her."

According to the Her Majesty's Secret Servant Web site, Hunt wanted to make sure Rigg and Lazenby would be compatible, so prior to offering her the role he took both actors out to dinner. As Hunt recalls, "I said to her, 'Now come on, I'm going to take you to dinner with George. I want you just to be with him and talk with him, we'll make it a perfectly sociable evening, but afterwards you have to tell me the truth, whether you think you can work with him and do the part.' I wouldn't have gone with him if Diana Rigg hadn't assured me that she liked him enormously at that time before we started shooting, and that she would do everything to help and work with him." The next day Rigg reportedly told Hunt, "No trouble at all. It will be marvelous," and accepted the role.

For Hall, Rigg was a coup. He explained: "Eighty percent of the film, any film, is casting. I insisted on having a very good actress, and got Diana Rigg. Even all the smaller parts were very good actors and that makes all the difference."

The plot of the film closely followed the book, in part because Hunt, who had been the editor on all the previous Bond films before taking over as director, wanted the film to be less gadget-heavy and more in keeping with the tone of the novel, considered by many to have been the best Bond adventure. "I aim to make people forget Connery as James Bond once they see Lazenby," he said.

Shooting began in October 1967 in Switzerland. The plot interweaves Bond's efforts to eliminate his arch nemesis, Ernst Stavro Blofeld, the evil mastermind behind the Spectre crime cartel, and his blossoming relationship with Tracy, the troubled daughter of a European crime boss named Marc-Ange Draco. Bond first meets Tracy when he saves her from committing suicide. They meet again in a casino, where Tracy

© BETTMANN/CORBIS

Rigg is the ultimate Bond Girl in *On Her Majesty's Secret Service*

claims to be a Contessa and runs up some big losses that Bond ends up covering. He finally discovers her true identity when her father has Bond brought to his office, where he makes the secret agent an offer: Draco will give him information of the whereabouts of Blofeld if Bond will protect Tracy. In fact, he offers James £1 million to marry his wayward daughter. Bond declines the marriage proposal but agrees to keep an eye on Tracy. As they follow Blofeld's trail, Bond and Tracy fall in love. After Tracy helps rescue Bond from Blofeld, he proposes to her and she accepts. Bond tracks down Blofeld, who is threatening to take over the world via biological warfare, and apparently kills him during a chase sequence on bobsleds. Bond and Tracy get married in a small Portuguese village then drive off to be alone. As they sit talking at the side of the road, a car driven by Blofeld drives by and his henchwoman, Irma Bunt, sprays Bond's car with a submachine gun. Bond is unhurt but Tracy is shot and killed. The movie ends with Bond holding his bride's lifeless body.

Because Lazenby was taking over for Connery, the media interest in the production was intense, with many second-guessing the producers' decision to cast an untried unknown. But the questions over his lack of acting credentials soon took a backseat to stories of trouble on the set. A story in *Family Weekly* painted an unflattering picture of Lazenby as an arrogant misogynist who seemed to relish his caddish behavior. According to the article, "One of the film's female stars recalls dropping a load of packages and having George practically walk over her without helping to pick them up." Some of the actresses on the film were also anonymously quoted as saying, "He's a brilliant conversationalist—as long as you want to talk about Australia," and, "He's only interested in sex"—a charge Lazenby denied.

As Lazenby tells it, "When I came to Murren (Switzerland) for location shooting, all the girls were chasing me. I can't really blame them, all they wanted was publicity, but sooner or later women become ugly and testy."

Lazenby also told Peer Oppenheimer that he wasn't at all stressed about stepping into the Bond role despite his lack of experience: "Bond is basically an arrogant, self-centered so-and-so, and that's the way I play him. When you come down to it, I'm really only playing myself." The producers learned early on that was indeed the case. To avoid any injury that could shut down production, Harry Saltzman told Lazenby he was not allowed to do any pleasure skiing during filming. But George ignored the order and flaunted his insubordination by skiing past the producer's window. "No one can make me do what I don't want to do," Lazenby challenged.

Whether it was genuine misunderstanding or arrogance on Lazenby's part is still debated today by Bond aficionados, but the end result was the same: tensions became so rigid on the set that George's relationship with the director and the movie's producers disintegrated. In a 1983 interview with *Starlog,* Lazenby admitted to feeling unappreciated. "I tried to get involved with the music, the direction and the writing," he asserted. "In 1967, I had an underground tape of Blood, Sweat and Tears before they even recorded an album. . . . Some guy laid it on me to introduce them to Broccoli. In July 1967, I was telling the producers about this group; when the film came out, in

1969, they had five hits. They said, 'Get out there, get on your marks, and do what you're told. We don't want you involved in any other areas.' I was trying to get away from what they were doing with Sean Connery. But they didn't want some new guy coming in and telling them how to run their show after they had been very successful at it for ten years before they even saw me." He said Broccoli and Saltzman "disregarded everything I suggested simply because I hadn't been in the film business, like them, for about a thousand years." He added, "They made me feel like I was mindless."

On the set, the long hours and intense pressure of making a film began to take their toll. Lazenby felt even more put upon and began to complain about his perceived slights in the press. George felt he was being alternately ignored and abused by Hall, who would later express bemusement. "I don't know why he should say that, because it's quite untrue," he said. "You can't possibly have a new, young guy who has never been an actor and not talk to him. You simply can't do it. I had to tell him where to go and what to do. The whole thing with him is that he changes his mind all the time. But he had to do what I wanted him to do. Indeed, we had long conversations during and before we even started shooting."

But Lazenby felt he was on an acting high-wire with no net, such as when it came time to film Tracy's death scene. "Read the last page of the book; that's what I did before I played that scene," he told *Starlog*. "I had nothing else to go on. I mean, no one was talking to me at that stage. The director and I hadn't spoken throughout the whole film. So, I was completely on my own and the only place I could get guidance was Fleming's novel. Everyone was upset with me because I didn't want to play Bond again."

Believing that starring in a Bond film would guarantee him offers to work in other films, Lazenby claims that midway through production, he made the decision not to return. "I mean, that was such a kick in the tails to their egos," he said. "They couldn't believe some actor wouldn't want to play James Bond, so they passed the word along that I was hard to get along with. The only way I was hard to get along with was that I wouldn't sign their contract. The contract was an inch and a half thick. It covered everything, from how to cut your hair to how to behave in public. When I read it, I said, 'Look, I'm not going to do all this for seven years, so count me out.'"

Hunt believed much of the drama was a direct function of Lazenby's emotional immaturity. He explained: "I think it's a measure of the man's personality. He changed about all over the place, when it all went to his head. You must remember that he was an ordinary little guy from the backwoods of Australia and he was suddenly thrust into a very sophisticated area of filmmaking, and it was very difficult for him.

"I had to do certain things that directors have to do. For instance, one of the best things he ever did was when she's shot. We got up there at eight in the morning, I insisted he was on set, I sat him in the car and made him rehearse and rehearse all day long, and I broke him down until he was absolutely exhausted, and by the time we shot it at five o'clock, he was exhausted, and that's how I got the performance. He thought that was me being unpleasant to him, but I couldn't say, 'Now, listen George, I'm going to do this because it's the best way to get you to react.' Maybe I did things like that all the way through, because I knew how to get emotions out of him, but he didn't seem to think that that was fair." Hunt would also note to Gary Giblin, "Well, you must remember that everybody's a little schizophrenic and actors perhaps more than others. And he was incredibly schizophrenic, really. He would be up and down all over the place. He needed managing. But I had to do that."

Although Lazenby himself would talk about his run-ins with Rigg, Hall, who died in 2002, always denied there had been bad blood between the two. The most infamous tale was when Lazenby told the press how Rigg had said she was eating "garlic with my pate" prior to a love scene. Rigg had been eating lunch in the commissary and was only joking, but the Fleet Street press ran with it, expanding it into a feud along the way. Hunt claims that while nobody would ever call them good friends, for the most part, Rigg and Lazenby got along fine off-camera. "No, there weren't really any fights," he told *Secret Intelligence.* "I mean once or twice he would get silly, but there were no fights. I mean, he had a great ego, which of course helped him. And there were one or two times when she began to think he was a bit foolish because he got a bit big-headed on occasion. But I expect that. I don't mind any of that. That's all human nature. I can cope with that in anybody. I wasn't worried by it. And Diana was a darling throughout the whole of the shooting. I loved her. I used to feed her with champagne, which she loved."

Of course, Rigg could afford to relax; she was a classically trained actress who had tackled some of Shakespeare's greatest dramas, so doing a movie didn't cause her any particular stress. For Lazenby, however, it was all a new experience. He frequently felt as if he were being patronized by members of the production team and his way of handling it was to lash out. While he might have had the looks and the physical prowess to play Bond, he lacked the emotional maturity to deal with the high-pressure world of moviemaking. Playing opposite the steady, self-assured Rigg must have made him feel that much more unprepared.

The movie was released in December 1969 and generated tepid audience reaction. Ironically, over the years, *On Her Majesty's Secret Service* has earned a legion of fans and is con-

Rigg at the London Hilton during a 1967 photo shoot

sidered by many to be one of the best in franchise history. While opinions on Lazenby still vary, Rigg's place in Bond lore is assured. Apollo Guide reviewer Dan Jardine notes: "Naturally our man Bond aims to thwart Blofeld's plans, but along the way 007 meets and falls for a fragile Italian Contessa named Tracy Draco, played with class and panache by the elegant and creamily beautiful Diana Rigg. Roger Ebert contends that it is the quality of the villains that determines the relative success of each Bond picture, and while this one certainly has a memorable villain, what secures its place at the fore of the Bond series is the role of Tracy and the performance of Rigg in that pivotal role. Tracy adds a layer of emotional complexity to the film that is otherwise unknown in a Bond film, and Rigg gives the most complex and compelling performance ever by a Bond girl."

James Berardinelli agrees: "The romance comprises most of the film's first forty-five minutes, as well as the final fifteen. For a series known for its action, the sensitivity of the James/Tracy pairing is surprising. Rigg does a marvelous job holding up her side, and after viewing her performance, it's not hard to understand how Bond could fall for the headstrong Tracy. Lazenby, on the other hand, manages to be merely adequate—this is the only occasion when a Bond woman upstages 007."

After the film's release, Lazenby and the producers waged a war of words in the trade press. George claimed it had been his decision not to do another Bond film despite being offered *Diamonds Are Forever*, while Cubby said Lazenby was not asked back. "Our parting was not by mutual desire, but by our desire," he asserted. "I wouldn't use him again, no. Why do we feel so strongly? Because he's a pain in the ass. I can tell you this in simple words. Life is too short to put up with an actor who is impossible, somebody who is not a pro. He is not a pro. You can quote me on that. I don't care. In the first place, to be a professional you have to get along with the crew and the people involved, and the producers, and everyone else. He was too much of a problem for us. He may be a genius to somebody else."

Even though the next film was scheduled to start production soon, Broccoli was unfazed by the prospect of finding yet another new Bond. "I must say, and I have always felt, that Bond is bigger than all of us," he said. "Bond is bigger than the directors, and the actors and the producers. I felt that way before we used Lazenby. To use an old bromide, Bond is like Tarzan and Sherlock Holmes, and all these things that have been going on for years. Bond is a very big, important name." Of course, Broccoli could afford to say that because he had managed to lure Sean Connery back to reprise Bond in the next scheduled film, *Diamonds Are Forever*, for a million-dollar salary.

Lazenby would accuse Broccoli of a simple case of sour grapes. Believing doing one Bond film would guarantee him steady film work, George says he quit to take advantage of these expected opportunities. But not right away. At first, Lazenby immersed himself in creature comforts, such as sailing trips aboard his new yacht. "I was offered a few films, like Italian westerns and what have you, and I could have gotten three times the amount of money they would have given me for a James Bond film, so I opted to get out of Bond and take those kind of offers, which," he admitted to *Starlog*, "never came around." Even if he had wanted to change his mind, he had so thoroughly ostracized himself, the breach was irrevocable. He explained, "By then Connery was back in the role, Roger Moore was waiting in the wings and Broccoli and Saltzman and I had all insulted each other in the press. So, there was small chance of me ever being Bond again. I didn't chase after it at all."

Lazenby accused Broccoli of bad-mouthing him to other producers. But the fact that *On Her Majesty's Secret Service* was the second-lowest grossing of the six Bond films up to that point didn't help his cause either. With jarring alacrity, Lazenby was off the public's, and Hollywood's, radar screen. "Within two years I didn't have a job, I had two kids, I was married and I was broke," he said. Unable to find work, he headed to Hong Kong, where he appeared in several kung fu movies. By 1973, Lazenby was a new father and blamed *On Her Majesty's Secret Service* for being a "total hindrance" to finding acting work in the U.S. "I didn't realize it at the time or I wouldn't have given up the role the way that I did," he remarked. "I would have continued to do it at least until I became a millionaire." Lazenby now jokes that he is best remembered as an answer to the trivia question, "Who replaced Sean Connery as James Bond?"

Since leaving Bond, Lazenby has had his share of personal and professional challenges. By far the most profound was losing his nineteen-year-old son Zachary to brain cancer in 1994. Although George has continued to act, he is still best known for the role he brushed aside. Today, he lives in California and is married to his second wife, former professional tennis player turned television analyst, Pam Shriver. Looking back at his opportunity lost, Lazenby's defense mechanisms take the edges of the what-might-have-been. He told *TV Guide* in 2002, "Time gets you over it. You look back and say, 'If I would have become James Bond for seven years what would have happened to me?' I probably would have had three wives in Beverly Hills, I'd probably be a dope addict. Anyway, I have a comfortable life. I've come through okay, but work isn't my life."

Shriver added, "Who is to say he didn't make the right decision? You never know where that kind of fame over a period of time can lead to."

Except for a rather arch letter to the editor refuting the story of her loading up on garlic, Rigg stayed above the fray. As always, she had theater to fall back on, and as soon as the last cork was popped at the *On Her Majesty's Secret Service* wrap party, Diana was already preparing for her next job, a star turn in a production of *Abelard and Heloise*, where once again she would leave the audience, and critics, with their tongues wagging.

CHAPTER NINE

• • • •

IN the twelfth century a philosopher, poet and theologian named Pierre Abelard was widely considered one of the most brilliant minds of his time. He worked at the University of Paris, and students all across Europe flocked to hear his lectures. He seemed destined for a great academic career—until he met an intellectually precocious seventeen-year-old named Heloise. She was the niece of Abelard's employer, Fulbert, a canon at the cathedral, who wanted Abelard to tutor Heloise. Although he was twenty-two years older than Heloise, Abelard found his soul mate in her, and their love affair would be both a great tragedy and a powerful example of enduring passion.

For a while, Abelard and Heloise successfully hid their affair from her uncle, who seemed oblivious to the rampant rumors swirling through Paris about the teacher and his special student. For his students, the change in Abelard was dramatic. Whereas in the past he burned with intellectual fervor, now all his attention and interest was focused on Heloise and his poetry turned into odes of love.

Their idealized existence came to an abrupt end when Fulbert discovered the affair by walking in and catching them *flagrante delicto*. The uncle tried to keep them apart, but when Heloise told Abelard she was pregnant with his child, Pierre stole her away from Fulbert's house and took her to his family, where she gave birth to a son they named Astrolabe. In an attempt to mitigate Fulbert's fury, Abelard offered to marry Heloise on the condition the ceremony be kept a secret.

While to modern sensibilities the reasons for keeping an affair secret might be understandable, keeping a marriage secret seems a bit unnecessary. However, at that time the most successful academics were single, in large part because they were in the clergy. The university where Abelard taught was an outgrowth of Catholic teaching institutions, so the fastest track and the greatest opportunities were still found in the Church. By forsaking the clergy and getting married, Abelard's career would effectively be over, which is why Heloise was against getting married. The marriage took place in spite of her objections, with Fulbert in attendance.

Abelard and Heloise continued their torrid relationship, prompting him to write, "In short, our desires left no stage of love-making untried, and if love could devise something new, we welcomed it." Except for Fulbert, the story of Abelard and Heloise might have ended there and evaporated into the mist of history. But the canon was determined to return Abelard to God and knew that would be impossible as long as he embraced pleasures of the flesh. Frustrated by Abelard's deceit, Fulbert decided to make sure their sexual relationship ended. Along with some hired enforcers, Fulbert burst into Abelard's room one night and castrated him. In the aftermath of the attack, Abelard wrote: "All sort of thoughts filled my mind—how brightly my reputation had shone, and now easily in an evil moment it had been dimmed or rather completely blotted out; how just a judgment of God had struck me in the parts of my body with which I had sinned."

But not even the end of the sexual intimacy dimmed Heloise's passion for Abelard. When he joined the Abbey of St. Denis, she took her own religious vows in order to be near him. During this time, they wrote letters to each other, many of which survive to this day and offer a glimpse into their extraordinary connection. When Abelard died, his body was brought to Heloise at the convent at Paraclete where he was buried. Six hundred and fifty years after their deaths, the French government ordered that their remains be buried together in the Parisian cemetery of Pere Lachaise. The site is marked with a headstone that reads: "Abelard : Heloise. Forever One."

In 1970, Diana agreed to expand her theater horizons away from repertory and into an extended run to star in Ronald Millar's play *Abelard and Heloise*. It doesn't take a psychologist's degree to understand why this story of true love in the face of impossible obstacles so appealed to Rigg or why she could tap into Heloise's ahead-of-her-time independence. "I like her because she has such integrity. She has a passion and she is single-minded about it," Rigg observed. "The church, of course, tried to distort that love in her. And it still does. I like her because she's inflexible. The modern idea of woman is not like that. Woman is supposed to be marriageable and fluid and soft. But I do not think passion is like that. Passion is single-minded."

To Rigg, Heloise's refusal to conform or compromise herself or her passion for Abelard was nothing short of heroic. "That is a dirty word now, but it should not be," she said. "To be heroic means not that you die in order to represent something, or even live in order to represent it, but that you just do represent it—be it. That is what Heloise does, very simply and directly. She is real to herself. And Heloise is truly romantic. Romantic does not mean all those Victorian things—flowers and embellishments. It means something pure and delicate and passionate. At the time of the play these things were terribly suppressed and even today with all our freedoms they remain as problems. Perhaps there are even greater problems since the laws and structures are falling. Law and the pressure of society are no longer imposing moral standards so now it must be imposed by the individual by his or her own personal definition of morality.

"It is a marvelous story and one I think of as a piece of theater—theater with a capital T. That kind of theater is always valid. It may not be the most valid, but it is always valid. It is a play that deals with the most fundamental things: mind, body and love."

As powerful a play as *Abelard and Heloise* was, it was actually the staging that had London abuzz when it opened at the Wyndham's Theatre. The play called for Rigg and her costar, Keith Mitchell, to appear nude for a brief but powerful love scene. It was the first time known actors in a major theater production had completely shed their clothes onstage. For all her sophistication, Rigg admitted exposing herself so completely for the love scene wasn't easy: "God, not with my background! It brought the world press to the theater on opening night. I was deeply uncomfortable. It was ghastly—so cold, awful. And, it never, ever got easier. Everybody thinks one enjoys flashing oneself on the stage and this is not true. I know it sounds like so much slush, but an actor does not serve himself; he serves the play. And I believe in nudity if it's vital to the text, and finally proved, to myself, that you don't have to have a perfect body to flash it. I mean, it does help, but it's not essential, and why should we all pretend that our bodies are the most sacred parts of us when they're not, absolutely not."

What bothered Rigg the most was her perception that the media were behaving like Peeping Toms. According to an article by Ronald Smith, Diana fumed, "All the press in London were down on us—most of them without having seen the play. *Hair* had already been in London with its nude scene but no one knew those kids and no one minded them undressed." Later, while guesting on Dick Cavett's talk show, she noted, "My body is no different from anybody else's. In fact, I remember one letter that said: 'I don't know why you bother. My girlfriend's tits are much larger than yours.' You see? But everybody who steps onstage has to have the definitive figure. But in the play, a definitive figure is neither here nor there—you're playing a character. You're fully dressed until the wings. Then you drop your knickers. That's easy.

Stepping onstage without your knickers is the most difficult thing in the world. I promise you, it is—if you've ever done it, it's against everything you've been taught. The press was there . . . panting, as if I had another breast and Mitchell had two penises."

However, most critics were able to look past the sensationalism and focus on her performance. The *Times* of London wrote about her performance: "It was gritty and aggressive, daring the house to laugh at lines, which from the mouth of a less assured actress would have provoked school-boyish titters."

Things weren't any easier when the play opened on Broadway. Acerbic critic John Simon took a cheap shot at Diana's physical appearance, saying she was "built like a brick mausoleum with insufficient flying buttresses." Although Rigg says she can laugh about the insult now, then the remark stung. "That hurt," she told Lawrence Eisenberg. "It's a physical attack on you and there ain't much you can do about that. I mean, if a critic sits down and says you're not good as an actress—which this man did subsequently do—because, because, because, well that's fine; you know where you're at and you can evaluate his criticisms. But to be physically attacked . . . ."

In an interview with Wayne Warga of the *Los Angeles Times*, Diana further observed: "I think that critics are really intimidated by success. Our situation in England is very different. For one thing, of course, we do not have any John Simon in England. He can be very, very harsh really. After his review came out I crept along the sidewalk for a couple of days disguised as somebody else. What you have among critics over here, there is a veritable frenzy on opening night. There are critics from radio, television and news services and then there is Clive Barnes. Collectively they serve as a sort of Nero. Thumbs-up and the play will flourish; thumbs-down, and it won't open a second night. See, you know within the hours of the early morning whether you're going to last or not."

However, Rigg also knew that critics were a vital cog in the theater machinery. "I don't mean to be oily," she said, "but critics are very much part of the theater. There are those who have a knowledge and passion for the theater, and those who don't. But they contribute to the body of literature that's written about the theater. We now depend on critics of the past to give us a flavor of what was going on then."

For as scathing as John Simon was, Clive Barnes, the *New York Times'* drama critic, was enthusiastic over *Abelard and Heloise* in general and Rigg in particular. He said Millar's "writing has more than a touch of wit, and here and there even flashes of real distinction to it." About Diana he said, "Miss Rigg has the more difficult role and was, I thought, perfect, as sensuous as a cat, with hidden fires beneath the surface, and a radiant beauty far more beguiling than that of many more obviously pretty women." He called the controversial love scene "the most tasteful, tactful, and apposite nude love scene I have ever encountered."

Barnes concluded: "This is, I feel, a rather better play than most of the London critics suggested but whether it will be able to repeat its huge public success in London will depend, quite possibly, on just how romantically inclined the Broadway public is right now."

The play was the first time Rigg had spent any appreciable time in the United States, and she found life in New York city "a bit overwhelming at first." Then she qualified, "But eventually, as one comes to think of it as a challenge and confronts the city on its own terms, one gets a sense of achievement, even triumph, here, which is unmatched anywhere in the world. New York is frightening, it is true. But it is also vibrant and alive and if you were going to have those qualities of vitality then there has got to be something on the other side of the ledger. The thing, finally, that makes New York worth it, is the people. They are more intense and dynamic and, I believe, creative."

While on Broadway Rigg was once invited to a party thrown by actress Eugenia Rawls where she was introduced to Alfred Lunt and Lynn Fontanne, actors widely considered the greatest acting team in the history of theater. Rigg cherishes the memory. "I just wanted to wrap them both up in cotton wool and take them away with me!" she exclaims.

On the Great White Way, Diana was much sought-after dinner company because she could regale people for hours with wonderful, occasionally risqué tales of the theater. One story in particular never failed to elicit shocked laughter. According to writer Ronald Smith, Rigg recalled one of her most vivid memories during her early days at the Royal Shakespeare Company playing Cordelia to Paul Scofield's King Lear. She explained how Scofield drank a health-food, high-fiber mixture of malt, bran, wheat and honey every day. "As a result, he suffered from flatulence," she recalled. "So odd sounds accompanied his impassioned cries of 'Howl,

howl, howl! O, you are men of stones.'" Diana says her biggest problem wasn't the aroma but of trying not to laugh in the scene where she lies dead in Scofield's arms.

But by the time Diana arrived in Los Angeles for the west coast run of the play, she had been doing the role for nine months and was feeling the strain. "I don't think I'll ever do this long run again," she told Wayne Warga. "It is dangerous in a lot of ways. The processes you go through are such that eventually you become a victim. I had only done repertory before this and now I find myself asking, 'Am I doing what I'm doing right? Can I improve it?' Then there comes a hot, sticky matinee and you walk through and it is deadly. Suddenly you're feeling very guilty. After the excitement of creating, what it boils down to—at least on certain days—is just doing. The key is to somehow avoid just doing, because it is dishonest to both yourself and your audience."

But for all her concern, Rigg's Heloise is now seen as one of the legendary roles in modern theater. She was honored as one of the year's best actresses by the London Critics' Circle and was nominated for a Tony as Best Actress in a Dramatic Play in 1971, losing out to Maureen Stapleton's turn in *The Gingerbread Lady*.

In addition to taxing her emotional and physical reserves, the long run of *Abelard and Heloise* sorely tested Rigg's patience with the media. Diana complained that when journalists asked her questions, "I answer honestly and directly but it's unreal." She went on, "Anything I say becomes a declamation. Publicity and being known and things like that are not important to me. Being real to myself is important to me.

I like playing Heloise because I can be onstage consistently what I would like to be in life all the time."

Diana understood the importance of doing publicity to promote a play and understood it was all part of the business of entertainment. She told a *Los Angeles Times* reporter in 1971, "In your way you represent a process, a form of authority and other things I do not comprehend or particularly like just now. It is a very suspect process to me. You ask questions; I answer; you write them down and then interpret them. That is almost a Chekhovian process. Meeting people and talking with them is great. But I am not about to reveal myself in any way and if I do, it will not be freely or of my own conscious choice.

"I think disrespect is a healthy act. It is much better than being subservient. You might say I'm disrespectful to the press, if only because it is an established process and I think it ought to be questioned."

Questioning institutions was the central theme of Rigg's next feature-film venture, *The Hospital.* Written by Paddy Chayefsky and directed by Arthur Hiller, the film starred George C. Scott as Dr. Herbert Bock, the chief resident at an overburdened New York City hospital. Overworked, reeling from the recent breakup of his marriage and suffering from impotence, Bock is a suicidal shell of his former, once highly respected self. And to top it off, patients in his hospital are dying at an alarming, and unnatural, rate. Rigg played Scott's opposites-attract love interest in this biting black comedy, a young free spirit named Barbara Drummond.

Diana says she came to be cast thanks to a play she had done in London years earlier: "George C. Scott saw me in the part. Then when they were working on the preparation for *The Hospital*, George asked me to meet Paddy Chayefsky, the writer, and I did. In the film I play an American girl, which is a bit presumptuous of me. Paddy said a curious thing, that he wanted an English actress to do it because we English are used to words and to the sound of words. We're used to dealing with them."

It's a measure of the respect Chayefsky generated that he was able to have so much control on *The Hospital*, considering that his film record had been spotty up to that point. He fought to have Scott cast as Bock when the studio, United Artists, pushed for more audience-friendly actors such as Burt Lancaster and Walter Matthau. Even though Scott's salary demands were at first refused, Chayefsky pressured the studio and the deal was eventually sealed.

The production got off to a troubled start when Chayefsky and first director Michael Ritchie fought over the set design. Once again, Paddy prevailed. Ritchie was fired and replaced with Arthur Hiller, who had worked with Chayefsky on *The Americanization of Emily*. Then, there was a disagreement over the casting of Barbara Drummond. Jane Fonda was originally on the shortlist but was harshly vetoed by Scott, who allegedly called her "still too much of a hippy, and in need of a bath." Ali MacGraw and Candice Bergen were also mentioned as contenders, but the person on top of Chayefsky's list was Diana Rigg, who initially passed, already overwhelmed by the grind of the play. But she was persuaded to reconsider after Barnard Hughes, who played Barbara's father in the film, paid her a surprise visit backstage after a performance of *Abelard and Heloise* and told her she would be missing an important experience if she passed up this opportunity. While he was referring to the positives of working with Chayefsky, he neglected to warn her about Scott's volatile personality.

The movie was filmed in New York at Metropolitan Hospital, and every day on the set was an adventure. Scott's home life with actress Colleen Dewhurst was going through a tense time and he was drinking heavily. There were mornings he would show up obviously hungover and/or inebriated, while on other days he didn't bother to show up at all. However, in that cosmic way that happens with certain actors in certain roles, Scott was able to channel all his inner turmoil into the character. He would eventually turn in a performance that would be widely regarded as one of his best, earning him an Academy Award nomination for Best Actor while Chayevsky won the Oscar for Best Screenplay.

In many ways, working on the film was an education. Although not everything Rigg learned was necessarily pleasant, it was useful nonetheless. "I think what happens in America is something which I personally have come to terms with," she told Richard Brown in 1972. "Success is considered of paramount importance here. If you are a success, you are working in making money, and particularly you're working in films. In America film seems to be a magic word. For example, in the film that I was doing, *The Hospital*, actors from the legitimate stage who would have only accepted major roles in stage plays would come in to do small parts, perhaps just a single line in the movie. They were delighted just to do the one line. So what we have is a major difference in attitude between the United States and England toward actors in general. I think the important part of it is that the whole mystique of being discovered in films is still perpetrated over here. In England, in order to be discovered in film, you have to be playing a sizable part."

In analyzing America's star system, Rigg observed, "Ironically, the same star system which many performers, including myself, have sort of become victims to has inverted itself. I have done some very mediocre films. They were extravagant, big-budget and rather poor for the most part. For me, because I have become, whether I like it or not, a success symbol, I never get offered an experimental film. Because of my image and perhaps my attitude or what people believe my attitude to be, suggests that I would not be interested in experimental, low-budget, non-Hollywood type of film. But given the opportunity I would be delighted if it is a good film, one which I could work in and really feel I was doing something important in." Diana looked with envy at actors who were part of a troupe, such as the kind Woody Allen or John Cassavetes assembled. She observed, "The way it is generally done in America is that when they do experimental film they just go out on the street and pick whoever strikes their fancy. It is rather sad for establishment figures like myself, whether we want to be establishment or not. As an actress I try to explore all areas and this is one area where the opportunity has never been given to me."

The Hospital was the first U.S. film Rigg worked on, and she was intrigued by the differences between American and English actors. "The advantage of being an English actor has a lot to do with tradition," she observed. "They are representative of years and years of working out a system. And of course the ensemble system in repertory renders everybody down to just being an actor in a company. We deal with words, and we know how to deal with words because of our heritage. But we're not so bright on the subtext level. We're really not. I admire American actors tremendously and I think Americans have evolved a very interesting system of acting because they probably had to deal with a load of crap in the past, and the really good actors evolved methods of filling that text and making it profound and interesting. The result is a very spare and economical style and truly American. It doesn't happen very often in England.

"It's a bit difficult to put one's finger on it but Americans also have a facility with emotions. They can go into and leave the emotions so quickly. Now, don't misunderstand because I'm not putting it down. English people tend to rely more on words and make the words do the work. Americans use their bodies, they use gestures, they use objects and they have a whole subtext going which, when it's good, is fantastic."

Nobody was more emotional that Scott, who Rigg admits was a bit intimidating. "He is so thoroughly professional," Diana marveled to Richard Brown. "And he knows what he is about, he knows what he has to do, and he goes about it in a way that's craftsman-like, even businesslike sometimes. Sometimes he might be impatient with the director. He likes everything to be done in one take. I'm fascinated by how George C. Scott works. He's incredible. He can snap on and snap off. No doubt it takes many years to develop this method of working and Scott can deliver on the instant. It takes me a while, but his first take is right on the head.

"I found it rather disturbing at first and I tried very hard to maintain an emotional level. I simply didn't have the time, I really didn't. We often have no time for rehearsals. It was on-off, on-off. It's really sort of, 'Okay, we're on. . . . You stand over here, you stand over there, know your lines.' Then we just go to it, as it is, which becomes frightening at times. I have to generate emotions immediately—there and then. So then, sadly, I fell back on the same technique that I used on the television series; if you can concentrate and if you can get it and if you are real there and then, it will work, at least in the context of that medium."

With her part in the movie over, when her run as Heloise ended, Diana returned to London and immediately jumped right into a new stage role. She joined the National Theatre in order to appear in Tom Stoppard's new play, *Jumpers*, and was reunited with Laurence Olivier, who at the time was the theater's director. Rigg and Olivier shared an affectionate mutual admiration. He called her "a brilliantly skilled and delicious actress." She told Lawrence B. Eisenberg that Olivier was "remarkable, as everybody knows." Then she added, "But were you to meet him you'd probably approach him with a great deal of reverence and you'd find he'd puncture that very quickly indeed. Because he's an irreverent man— thank God. Enormous fun."

Even so, Rigg observed to Richard Brown that as she had grown older and gained more experience, her perception of his work had subtly changed: "The last time that I saw Olivier was when he was playing with the National Theatre. The first time I saw him was when he was playing Coriolanus and I had a walk-on part. The very things I found impressive the first time I saw him were the things that, when I saw him last, I found the least moving and the least admirable."

But her memories of Olivier, the man, were untarnished. Diana laughingly recalled one of their more amusing encounters: "I remember a run-through when I was doing Lady Macbeth for him at the Old Vic. At the end of it we all expected some words of wisdom from him because he knew a very great deal about the play. And we all thought, *'Well, now we're going to hear where it's all at.'* Instead of which, there was total silence. He called across at me and said, 'Uh, Diana, you weren't wearing a bra in that run-through, were you?' And I said, 'No.' And he said, 'Very disturbing.' And that's all the notes I got on Lady Macbeth!

"And I fully understood the implication of that. He didn't know where to start! I was so terrible that he felt it was much better to finesse the whole issue, and that set up a great sort of relationship. On the night I opened in *Pygmalion* I got a message from Sir Laurence. It said: 'Tits won't help you in this part.' And he calls me 'Tits Rigg,' which is crazy, because I don't have those—I'm not known for my tits."

But she *was* getting quite a reputation for shedding her clothes. Right on the heels of Heloise's nudity, Rigg was at it again in *Jumpers*, in which her character, Dottie, also has a brief nude scene. "Well, doing *Jumpers* wasn't so hard," she demurred. "Actually, I started on a bed nude and very quickly put a sort of dressing gown on." In any case, Diana saw "no point in being defensive about eroticism." She said in a *Maclain's* interview, "I think it's rather good to have it. But if people care to see me as a sex symbol then they'll have enormous problems confronted with me."

The biggest problem for Rigg in *Jumpers* wasn't the lack of clothes but just trying to understand the play. Although it defies easy explanation, in general the play is about an academic named George and his wife, Dottie. George is writing a lecture on the existence of God while Dottie is lamenting the fact that men have landed on the moon, thereby destroying its special, mystical significance. Stoppard is an exceedingly cerebral playwright, and his complex plays demand uncommon attention. "I didn't understand it at first. Nobody did," Rigg admitted to Margaret Tierney. "Tom came over to see me and spent two hours making a path in the carpet telling me what it was all about. Tom's an incredibly brilliant man. In terms of the theater he's years ahead of anyone else I've ever read. Everything in this play is perfectly logical. Everything ties in, but it doesn't tie in the sequence that we, as theater-people, you as theatergoers, are used to. Tom expects his audiences to lean forward in their seats and take note of absolutely everything because, in order to understand the play, it is necessary. If you miss the clues your enjoyment is halved."

By 1972, Diana Rigg had a solid, thriving career. But her personal life was going through upheaval. Part of it was adjusting to the death of her father from cancer in 1971, something completely out of her control; part was facing the inevitable conclusion of her long-term affair with a married man, something very much in her control. Although she had been heartfelt all those years when saying she had to live her life the way she saw fit without worrying about "other people's social consciousness," Rigg knew the time had come for a change. Diana finally had to face the reality that her emotional life was spinning its wheels, and the only way to move ahead was to break free from the relationship that was stifling her personal growth. After eight years of defending her choice of living with a married man, Diana ended the relationship. "Yes, I took the first step. I had to, even though I think he would have realized it sooner or later," she told *Oui*.

"You can't get it right," she explained. "There is no point when you can finally say, 'I got it right.' Of course you get it right day-by-day, at times. We got it right, but eventually we got it wrong. There's no ultimate right. To have survived eight years together means that you got it right at some point. That's more than a lot of people do. But we both failed. Unquestionably we both failed. And it was facing up to the fact of failure which was really extremely hard. By way of softening the blow, I told him before I left that there was nobody else. The conversation went as follows:

'I have to go. I don't think it's working anymore.'

'I am very insulted.'

'There is nobody else.'

'I am very, very insulted.'

"A most wonderful conversation, it sums up the whole male attitude towards this. For 'insulted' read 'bewildered and hurt, but I'm not going to let you know.'"

In the immediate aftermath of the breakup, Rigg thought the traditional anticipation of finding a lifelong mate was misguided. "They got it wrong," she said. "That's an ideal, and if it occurs then it's well-nigh a miracle—which doesn't mean it can't occur. It can, but on average it doesn't. There are other people who can make it work by sheer willpower, the sheer fact that they will not accept defeat. It's just like anything else—familiarity is a very strong pull."

One question that seemed to float to the surface during many interviews was whether or not Rigg had hopes of being a mother. Now in her thirties, which for that era was late in life for a woman to still be single and without a family, Rigg was often put on the defensive. "About having the baby—I do not know," she declared. "It's always rather ridiculous and hypothetical to talk about it. I have not done it. I am not married. I see no reason to get married, so far. So how do I see having a baby? I don't know. Ask me when I've got it all planned, on a point of doing it. It is easy enough to conceive, there, after the most painful part of my eight-year relationship was living with Philip and knowing that it had to finish. That was really agony. Once the split happened, life was comparatively easy."

Breaking away from Philip prompted Diana to reassess her life. "I am very committed to acting while I am actually doing it," she told Winifred Blevins. "But I do not know what I will do next or whether I will always act. I think I can do other things and I would like to. We have a luxury in this business of being out of work from time to time. I want to take advantage of it to think about where I am. I think that one should not move forward until one is fully aware of where one is." She added to Wayne Warga, "I never plan things too far in advance, and when I am making up my mind I consider my immediate past. I am always looking to do something which contrasts with what I have recently done. I look for contrasts and then act on them. No great cerebral process, just an instinct to do different things."

Suddenly finding herself unattached gave Rigg a certain sense of freedom, as well as a vague rootlessness. She explained, "An actress never really settles anywhere, you know? If you act then you go to where the work is. A greengrocer can set up shop just about anywhere he cares to, but an actor must live where his job takes him. Insofar as I have a home base, it will always be England. But my real home will be wherever there is work that I find challenging and important."

But just when Rigg was rediscovering how to be alone, she was blindsided by an unexpected fresh start.

CHAPTER TEN

• • • •

W H E T H E R symbolic of a fresh start or just a case of upward mobility, Rigg moved out of the house in St. John's Wood where she had lived with Saville and moved into a small rental house located in Barnes that came with "a lovely English garden." Diana said of her new garden, "Divine. I have planted some lupins in the garden, the flowers of one's childhood." The only downside was that the house lay in the flight path of an airport. "It is a disgrace the way they jettison fuel before landing," Diana noted. "I don't think people are aware how much they are shat upon."

While many people would turn to friends for a shoulder to cry on in the aftermath of ending a long-term relationship, Diana remained in emotional solitude. "I am told I am too independent," she acknowledges. "It's a fault when you can't say, 'Help,' but all I can do is to retire and get solitary and work things out for myself." Puttering around her new house was cathartic for Rigg and she also found the house's location soothing. "Barnes is near Richmond and its park," she explained. "It's practically in the country. I was born under a water sign, Cancer, so I love the water very dearly. I often walk by the Thames and it gives me much solace. When I was doing Lady Macbeth for the National, I learnt most of my lines on its banks. The ducks used to get 'I have given suck . . .' at least once a day."

Traveling with *Abelard and Heloise* had given Rigg a fresh perspective on her adopted city: "I love London—it's such a familiar city and I think that's ninety percent of the joy of it. Because it's so familiar, I can feed whatever appetite I want whenever I want. I know exactly where to go for this or this or this. Now I'm in what you might call London's countryside on the west side of the city. However, I still come in to shop

© BETTMANN / CORBIS

Diana Rigg in costume for *Theatre of Blood*

in Soho—I often bring a shopping bag and do the markets before the matinee. There are marvelous butchers, and Spanish and French shops, and for a sandwich I often stop in at one of the salt-beef bars. Anyone coming to London shouldn't miss Soho—even if they are just going to look—because it's so special."

Rigg had been working so much that her

house was a bit on the spare side when it came to furnishing. "I haven't got much so far—the dining room table or chairs, no teacups," she said. "I am not at that level yet. Mugs. While I am away I will probably let friends stay in it; mug-holding friends."

In 1972, Diana began work on a new film project, one that craftily combined her classical background within a horror setting. *Theatre of Blood* was notable both for its surprisingly literate screenplay and for its star, Vincent Price. "I did it for fun," explained Rigg, "because it appealed to my sense of humor and I had no idea it was going to be so enormously enjoyable, which it was, mainly because of Vincent, who is heaven." In *Vincent Price: A Daughter's Biography* by Victoria Price, Rigg also says of the script: "It struck me as witty and wonderful and funny to be doing the classics on one hand and a spoof of the classics on the other."

Rigg says, "I didn't meet Vincent before we started working, so we were thrown into the deep end together in a way. We hit it off immediately. I had met several other horror-movie actors. They take themselves so seriously and I wondered what Vincent Price would be like. The first morning I met him in make-up and he was complaining about a mustache. 'It looks like a bunch of pubes up there,' I heard him say. He is so kind and intelligent—and has a filthy sense of humor." Needless to say, he was Rigg's kind of costar. "I worshiped Vincent," she said. "What people don't know unless they have seen the film, and tend to forget because of his horror movies, is what a great classical actor Vincent was. He was wonderful. In the film, he had these excerpts from all these plays, and he did them so wonderfully. It was a great loss that, in later life, he never did some. I think he would have been a great Lear. A great Lear. He just didn't take himself seriously. Listening to him deliver some of those Shakespearean speeches, I remember thinking, *'God, what a missed opportunity.'"*

The St. Louis-born Price admitted he would have liked the opportunity to show off his skills beyond horror films but added, "You know, I don't think we do Shakespeare as well as the English do. We just don't. It's their language. They attack a Shakespearean part, like a piece of music. They understand Shakespeare; he wrote for them, we just borrow it."

The movie is basically a sequel to Price's 1971 film, *The Abominable Dr. Phibes,* in which he played a deformed madman who goes around killing his enemies out of revenge. American International Pictures used that same revenge-killings formula for *Theatre of Blood,* but thanks to the inventive screenplay, the movie rose above its expectations and became a cult classic. In the film Price plays a scene-chewing Shakespearian actor named Edward Lionheart who murders his critics, one by one, using methods he appropriates from Shakespeare's dramas. Rigg plays his equally demented makeup artist daughter, who helps him carry out the killings.

Price's melodramatic turn as Lionheart and his reputation as a "horror actor" masked the fact that he had once been leading-man material. Over the years his style of acting had fallen out of favor. "During the great heyday of movies there were these great romantic overtones to the pictures," he observed to Lawrence French. "Then suddenly in the fifties, a whole new group of actors came out—Marlon Brando, James Dean and Paul Newman—who were very moody and realistic. So actors like myself and Basil Rathbone and so on didn't really fit into those realistic dramas and we began to do costume pictures. This was really the only place we could go on working if we wanted to survive as actors."

Directed by Douglas Hickox and written by Anthony Greville-Bell, *Theatre of Blood* is a dark-comedy horror extravaganza that bubbles over with Shakespearian references as it incorporates death scenes devised by the Bard. It includes some from his more obscure plays, like *Titus Andronicus* (a critic is force-fed to death with a baked pie made with his two pet poodles) and *Cymbeline* (a critic is decapitated in his bed). Proving once again it really is a small world after all, the only critic to survive is played by none other than Ian Hendry, John Steed's original partner on *The Avengers*.

Price said *Theatre of Blood* was one of his favorite films "for a lot of reasons, one being the premise of it, which is really hysterically funny." He explained, "The cast of critics were really extraordinary. They were all major actors in England—Jack Hawkins, Robert Morley, Arthur Lowe, Ian Hendry. It was wonderful, except it was kind of embarrassing, because between them all, they had done every single play of Shakespeare's on the stage. I think a lot of them had seen the *Dr. Phibes* films, which were very popular in London, and they all kind of wanted to be in one of these crazy pictures that I do. The picture was worked around their schedule because a lot of them were doing plays in the West End. They drove out to the studio, which was about an hour outside of London, did their day's work, then went back to the stage." Regarding the film's ongoing appeal, Price observed in the early 1990s, "It's really become a cult film, which is sort of fun, except you begin to feel like a cult yourself."

The movie was shot on location in London. While some of the settings were spectacular, Rigg and Vincent wondered more than once if their own safety was at risk. "The theater where I have my company, and where I lure all the critics to come and then murder them, was the Putney Hippodrome," Price recalled. "It was a great place that was going to be torn down. It had really fallen into decay and was a very dangerous place to work. We really shouldn't have been in it." Another scene was shot at an abandoned wine warehouse, which Price recalled was "almost under the Thames River." He explained, "It had been abandoned for a long time, and had great drips of water that made these stalactites, and it was pitch black. They lit it with a thousand candles, which made it a very spectacular scene. You could never build a set to look that way in a hundred years!"

In the end, the film would be most notable for Price on a personal level, because it's where he met Coral Browne. Price told Lawrence French about the first night he and Rigg had dinner together prior to filming: "She said, 'I hear you're going to meet Coral Browne tomorrow.' And I said, 'Yes, I am, and I'm quite anxious about it, because I hear she's a woman with a tongue like a lash!' So Diana said, 'Well you be sure and say hello to her for me, and take down everything she says, because she's supposed to be so funny.'

"The next day when I was introduced to her I said, 'Hello, Miss Browne, Diana Rigg told me to take down everything you say, because you're so witty,' whereupon she shut her mouth and never opened it again!" However, it was apparent to those working on the film that there were some underlying sparks between Price and Browne. But when filming ended, they went their separate ways. However, their pending romance was spurred on by Diana, who adopted the role of matchmaker by reuniting them after the filming at a charity event. After that nudge, the two actors began dating, and eventually Browne became Price's third wife. They were together until Coral's death in 1991. A grieving Price died two years later.

To this day, Rigg says her most vivid memories from the movie "are Vincent's tortured feet." She explains, "During the course of the film, Vincent was often in costume appropriate for delivering a lot of the very famous Shakespeare soliloquies. As a result of his foot problems, he would always find out if the next shot was a long shot, medium or close-up. If it was medium or close-up, he'd clamber into the oldest pair of carpet slippers I have ever seen. My problem was to keep a straight face looking at Vincent delivering these soliloquies sublimely in costume, with his feet in those carpet slippers."

For as well as they got on personally and professionally, Price was also a perfectly suited costar for Diana because of his 6'4" height, which meant Rigg wouldn't have to slouch to try and minimize her own height. Back in 1967 the *Toronto Telegram* had written: "The only thing that can keep Diana Rigg from becoming an international film star is the shortage of tall leading men. She insists that she is just 5'8½", but anyone who has seen her television series, *The Avengers*, will note that wearing sandals she is eye-to-eye with her co-star, Patrick Macnee. And Macnee is 6'1".

"Miss Rigg has heard all the usual horror stories tall girls are told when Hollywood makes its offers: How Ingrid Bergman (5 feet 10) had to stand in a hole in the ground for love scenes with one famous star and how another name celebrated on motion picture theatre marquees climbed on a box to kiss her tenderly in another film. If an actor can't stand on his own two feet to kiss Miss Rigg they are either going to have to get another actor or cut out the love scenes. In her early career as a Shakespearean actress she had all the sloping about with bent knees she is ever going to do. From now on she is going to look the world right in the eye—and a tall world it will have to be."

Staying true to form, Diana went back to the boards after finishing *Theatre of Blood*. "The National has been marvelous," she enthused in 1973. "On the good days I think how lucky I am—Lady Macbeth, *Jumpers* and *The Misanthrope*—where else could I do that? But you could get knocked out when you are rehearsing a new production and acting at night. I think ninety percent of a good performance—and I know this is a generalization—is energy. I literally give a good performance if I have energy to spare and I have a real relish for what I am doing."

At the time, Diana was relishing her work and her cadre of friends, most of whom were not fellow actors. She explained, "I am an actress but I spend time with people who do things that I don't do, like write, like compose, like paint, whenever—as long as they don't do what I do and they know more about it than I do. I am an avid taker, I suppose. In this business there is an awful lot of time you spend pleasing people, because that is what the business is about, but in that process you can very easily lose a sense of your own tastes and directions. A medium has to be found, and it disturbs me if I'm not keeping that balance."

For Rigg, part of the balance of her professional life was to never shy away from a challenge, regardless of where it might take her. In July 1973, it took her to Hollywood, where she began production on her own American television series. Although starring in a sitcom hadn't been part of any master plan, Rigg simply felt the time was right to take the plunge. She explained: "I am involved in all media of acting. I'm bred in the theater. I do my best work in the theater. But I'm in a profession that exists in many forms. I must move in them all, to keep assuring myself I can do the work. If I can turn my hand to all of them, I'll consider myself an actress. I'm not one of those people who consider television to be the bastard child of film. Television is an important medium. Why wouldn't I want to involve myself? I want to go to America because American television is an incredibly powerful arena. I'm not after power but the experience of it. It will not be the end-all and be-all. What I do here is more important to me."

Besides, as she noted, "I'm being absolutely practical. American bus drivers make more than I make at the National Theatre." Her stipend at the time was $175 a week, plus a performance fee of seventy-five dollars a week during the run of the play. "I do fourteen [episodes] and then they decided whether to take up the option," she explained. "If they do the whole series it will make me rich. If they don't I have still made enough to buy a house of my own in London. If I did everything for some sort of artistic justification, I could only work for half my life."

Rigg has often commented on how it is considered bad form in England to discuss money. "It's not really a socially correct subject, and mostly for this reason you hire an agent to discuss it for you. It is rather like sex in this country," she observed. But the stark reality was—and still is—that theater actors were by far low men on the salary totem pole. While actors may do theater for their artistic souls, they also need to do television and film to support their stage habit. Up until the U.S. series, Rigg had never managed to consistently hit big paydays. "In *The Hospital*, even though it was a three-million-dollar movie, I earned less than I earned on the Bond picture," she said. "What they tell you is, 'Well, we will defer so much.' It so happens that deferment is often Never-Never Land."

The series started with an idea. After rejuvenating her theater soul with performances in *The Misanthrope* and *Jumpers*, Diana says, "I realized I wanted to do more TV. I was always being offered formats over there. Sir Lew Grade once offered me six at a time, but they each started off, 'Entered Diana Rigg, gun in hand. . . .' It was at that point that I decided I would write my own format. I wanted to do a western TV series because I was devoted to my father and he loved westerns. I wrote one that was a gentle satire about an English woman coming into a western town and satirized their male-oriented society." Diana sent her idea to producer Leonard

Stern, whom she had met two years earlier and who had previously executive produced several hit series, including *Get Smart* and *McMillan and Wife*.

Stern liked the idea enough that he flew Rigg to Hollywood for a meeting. However, Diana would soon learn that nothing was straightforward in the world of U.S. network television. She explains, "We met with the networks and decided upon NBC, and that was where I first heard the word demographics. NBC said, demographically speaking, westerns were dead. Would I consider another format? I would. NBC then told Leonard that he should come up with three formats and let me choose one of them. They showed me three other ideas, and I liked this one, an English girl alone in America." Rigg thought the setup allowed her to be herself: "I am using what I am familiar with. We examine all sorts of attitudes, English and American. We can satirize them. We look at my femaleness and my Englishness, as opposed to their American counterparts."

The show would be called *Diana* and in the blush of the optimism that always envelopes productions in the beginning, Stern and Rigg shared their mutual delight. The producer told *TV Guide*, "Diana is bright and knowledgeable. She is like the leading ladies of the 1930s and 1940s. She's the mucilage of the show."

Rigg responded by saying she had trust in Leonard's guidance: "I feel safe in his hands." Stern's idea was to have Diana "reacting to oddball characters who are really doing cameo appearances," and the idea of being straight woman appealed to Rigg. "I prefer it that way," she said. "I'm not

Lucille Ball. I prefer the business of the subtle reaction. You have marvelous character actors and actresses in America and I have always felt that they are the prop and stay of any show. I cannot do it myself. I need help."

Once the deal was signed, Rigg was left with the reality of actually having to relocate to Los Angeles for the next six months, a prospect which she found somewhat daunting. "Apart from anything else, there's just the work of shutting up the house, the sheer hassle of getting myself and my goods over there," she told Tom Lambert of the *Los Angeles Times*. "I'm English and the English rhythms are my rhythms and suddenly I've got to adapt to a new society and new rhythms and I don't know how easy that will be. Here, I can go anywhere I want here, feed whatever appetite I want to feed. But I've got to start afresh in Los Angeles and find out where to feed my appetites, whether for beautiful pictures, to buy books, to sit with friends and talk, to walk alone. I know exactly where to go here to do those things, but not there." As if giving herself a mental slap, she added, "The contemplation may be much worse than the actuality; it usually is."

One previous experience in Los Angeles had stuck in her mind and left her with the sensation of the City of Angels being a very lonely place. She recalled to *Los Angeles* magazine an encounter she once had with a stranger: "I like to walk alone and I was walking one day along the strip near the Chateau Marmont when a man joined me and asked if we could talk. So I said sure. Maybe it was because I seemed sympathetic, but suddenly it all came pouring out—his problems with the family, with his wife and in his job. He must have talked for at least fifteen minutes and I found myself making suggestions. I really felt sorry for him. It must be hard sometimes here to find an ear you can bend."

Another part of her anxiety was that it was one thing to go to New York and appear in a play that people come to watch but quite another to do a series where you need to be welcomed into the viewers' homes. It made Rigg contemplate the drawbacks of playing for what for her was a foreign audience. "I really know so little about America," she admitted. What little she did glean was from working on Broadway. "New Yorkers are very facile," she observed. "I'm not that facile. I find myself guarded and suspicious. The American people do come toward you. They're open and friendly. I'm from more northern climes. I take longer to warm up."

Some of what she had seen during her time in New York had left her troubled. She mentioned to *TV Guide*, "I lived in Greenwich Village in the summer of 1971. It was very disturbing to see the young people on drugs, people dropping on the street, nobody helping them. And the mugging . . . ." And being a product of socialized medicine, she once commented, "It's unbelievable you have to pay for blood transfusions here."

Some of the perks being offered her by the network were equally unbelievable. She recalled getting a phone call, "saying they found a beautiful house for me in Benedict Canyon but it did not have a swimming pool." She added, "I did have the grace to smile to myself when I said I *must* have a swimming pool. Sitting in Barnes it was all rather difficult to envisage."

Even more difficult for Diana was adjusting to the unique lifestyle embraced by denizens of sprawling Los Angeles. Her first complaint was typical: "In London, I could walk anywhere. In Hollywood nobody walks. Hollywood is not cosmopolitan. People here are so square—they play tennis and jog. I'll have to create my own milieu and move inside it." She was also bemused by some of the programming on U.S. airwaves: "Absolutely amazing, those Marathon ladies on roller skates, Amazons, they were having fisticuffs. But I mean what kind of person are they—what kind of sexual undertow is there?"

Once production got underway, Rigg was forced to set aside her fascination with the unanswered mysteries of roller derby and concentrate on her own character. In the series she plays Diana Smythe, a recent divorcée who has come to New York for a fresh start. She works as a fashion coordinator at Buckley's Department Store and is staying at her brother's apartment while he is out of town—a brother who has a startling number of friends who all seem to have keys to his bachelor pad. The revolving door was set up as a running gag that would allow for a string of cameo appearances.

It was inevitable that any sitcom about a single, professional woman looking to find her way would be compared to *The Mary Tyler Moore Show*, which at the time was going into its fourth season and was already a top-ten hit. Rigg preferred not to know. "Ever since I first arrived here everybody has been telling me to study *The Mary Tyler Moore Show*," she remarked. "I have not seen it and I am not going to watch it because I don't want to be affected by it. She's enormously successful but I want to do my own thing. I know if I watched it I could learn many technical things that I don't really know yet. But that knowledge will come with doing my own show. Learning about sitcoms carries a fascination for me. I know I'll love doing it. I see the show as a progression. I don't ever want to reach a peak, because it's all down thereafter, isn't it?" The other thing that gave Rigg pause was the long-term commitment a U.S. series demands. "I've got the next year mapped out for the first time in my life," she said. "Actors and actresses should not map out too much. It is not what our business is about."

While the series was clearly a vehicle for Rigg, she was adamant that it be an ensemble show. She explained: "You'll have noticed that the actors and actresses who work with me in the series are brilliant, the best there are at that type of humor. I play straight man to them and that's the way I want it because I'm learning. I am learning timing and inflection, which are both very different in America. I know nothing about the technical side of things; I only know that there are things I must learn and conquer, and I like that. I'm learning the three-camera technique in front of a live audience, which I have never done before. And I am learning American comedy, which seems to me to be infinitely more lively than British and more subtle once you're into it." Not feeling confident in American pop culture made Diana feel ill equipped to offer too many opinions about the early scripts. "I'm in a cleft stick," she said. "I don't understand America, so I can't say how anything will go over with an American audience. They told me I would have to be vulnerable and understandable because it would be aimed at Middle America."

After she got past the first episode, Rigg felt a sense of relief. "I wasn't so much nervous as I was concerned with all the technical things," she noted. "I could not enjoy myself as much as I usually do. But I feel that I'm getting right into the swing of how things work." The worst part of sitcom life for Diana was the hours. Being a theater person and a natural-born night person, getting up for early set calls left Rigg cranky. "It's an outrage to sit in a makeup chair at 8:00 A.M. and have somebody make up your face," she griped to *TV Guide*. "It's almost obscene. You've just got up; you're at your most tender and vulnerable. My face doesn't take kindly to makeup at 8:00 A.M."

Her favorite part was that the show filmed before a live audience. "I know more about theater than movies or television and I feel more at home in it, more in control, and because of the interplay with the audience, with other actresses and actors. The thing about this television series, it combines theater and television beautifully, in fact like doing repertory," she explained. The schedule wasn't too demanding, either. "I get the weekends off, and every eight weeks they give me a fortnight's holiday," she said. "I may want to go to Mexico City. I've always wanted to go there and travel around a bit."

As Rigg started doing publicity for the show, she caught some journalists off guard with her candor. When asked to describe herself by *Los Angeles* magazine in 1973, Rigg didn't miss a beat: "The shoulders are extremely wide and very square, and the breasts don't compensate for this width. The hips are too wide. The arms and wrists are slender, but the knees are those of a hockey player and the calves are overdeveloped. The jaw is much, much too strong and the mouth is too small." During the photo shoot, she also joked, "How does *Los Angeles* magazine feel about nipples? I am not wearing a bra and this sweater's a bit thin. NBC doesn't like nipples at all, or navel, or any manifestation of humanity."

However, she showed a tinge of exasperation when besieged with questions that had dogged her since *The Avengers:* Why would one of England's best stage actresses go slumming on TV, particularly on an American sitcom? She responded: "Why I am doing this and Laurence Olivier is selling cameras on television is something English people understand but Americans never do. It has to do with your being a professional practicing your profession. We simply don't have that status hang-up. The theater no longer breeds its own stars. They must come from outside. For a time, they came from movies, but today they come from television. I am valuable to the National Theatre not only as an actress but because people know me from *The Avengers*; they come to see Mrs. Peel. With the importance of the tourist audience, it is important Americans know you. And the best way is through television."

Diana was also intrigued at how television created an environment where actors were often seen as so much fluff. "Because I did Shakespeare for five years I was always taken seriously," she explained. "The parts for an actress in the theater are excellent. I was lucky enough to have people believe in me at a young age, but I must say that an actor must have a sense of personal value. I'm not talking about ego but value

Rigg with Patrick Macnee when he guest-starred on her TV series, *Diana*

of himself, or herself, as an actor. If the TV show does not go here I will just get on a plane and go back to England where my career is entirely separate. I'll go right back to the National Theatre. I do not mean to sound arrogant but it gets back to having that sense of value. American actors let anxieties creep in. They must learn their value. If you are an actress, you're expected to be . . . stupid, vain. Well, we are intelligent. The nature of our work demands it. I'm not exactly all teeth and tits, am I?" Nor was Rigg worried about competing with Hollywood starlets. "I am honest about my age," she told the *New York Times*. "I am not interested in chasing youth. When I play eighteen- and twenty-year-olds, I throw myself on the mercy of the audience."

Unfortunately, television viewers and critics showed little mercy. *Diana* premiered September 10, 1973, and from the outset, the show was in trouble. *TV Guide's* review was typical: "So that is Diana Rigg, who not too long ago was doing Shakespeare, Molière and Tom Stoppard on successive nights in London, and is now doing the three-camera bit at Studio City. It baffles some. A veteran Hollywood observer says, 'If you can imagine Mary Tyler Moore playing Lady Macbeth or Sandy Duncan doing Molière, then you can picture Diana Rigg in this silly sitcom. I can't. It's like drinking coffee in London. Worse. It's like drinking tea in the States.'"

Rigg recalls that another writer "called it 'as light and frothy as a large glass of prune juice.'"

Poor reviews and a tepid audience response spurred producers to retool the show on the fly. One curious change was a switch from film to tape. They also wrote in fewer slapstick gags and tried to up the wit quotient. They also brought in older romantic interests, including some stunt casting with Patrick Macnee, who played a concert pianist who was Diana's former lover.

Initially, Rigg had deferred to the writers, feeling unqualified to challenge them on what the viewers would find funny. But when it became apparent the show's survival was at stake, she became more vocal. She explains, "I will take some credit. I suppose I should have stuck my oar in earlier. But all my training taught me to do what I was told and keep my mouth shut. What we were doing was obviously not working and I began to think that, after all, I had been rattling around the world for thirty-five years and I had picked up ideas that might help.

"I finally spoke up when we were reading the script in which a woman rises from an affair and tells her lover, 'Thank you.' I said no woman would do that. We got into a violent argument, an absolute brawl, and the more we argued, the funnier it got. Finally Leonard Stern, the producer, said, 'Let's throw away the script and shoot the argument.'"

Unfortunately, the show was past saving. NBC chose not to pick up the option for the second half of the season, and the last episode aired January 7, 1974. Rigg refused to hang her head and assessed the experience with as objective an eye as possible. "The trouble was not the show, it was me," she said. "They tried to make it more meaningful—a word I loathe— but they did not know what to do with it, nor did I. Actually, I learned quite a lot. I learnt that I cannot be funny without a good script, that I cannot conjure comedy out of nothing the way some great comedians can because I am not inherently funny. And I do not have the courage for pratfalls. I have to apply the standard of literacy of my stage work to the rest. I'll have to be more choosy.

"There's no way to ignore the fact that it was just one of those things that didn't work. I saw the pilot and thought there were possibilities. There was a big splash about me going there—and then there was a dreadful thud as the show hit the floor. It was just a big nothing. Ninety percent of Hollywood television is the offspring of a past success, and this one was daughter of *Mary Tyler Moore*, although I didn't know it at the time."

In some ways, Rigg believed that the cancellation was probably for the best in the long run. The thought of living in Los Angeles for an extended period of time was hard for her to fathom. "It wasn't just the Hollywood atmosphere, it was the life," she explained to the *Times*. "It isn't a life. People aren't aware how much private lives in Hollywood are sacrificed on the altar of career. You leave the house at 6:30 in the morning and work until 6:30 at night. If you are doing a series it goes on and on forever. I suspect I would not have stayed even if *Diana* had been a success. I truly don't think I would have been beguiled by the money. There should be more to one's life than that."

The perfect exclamation point on her Los Angeles experience was the not-so-subtle dismissal given her by the network: "When I arrived in Los Angeles, the studio sent this three-block-bus, smoked-glass limousine to meet me. Six months later, the day I left, they sent the banged-up studio station wagon. I never stopped laughing on the plane home. 'You've failed,' they were telling me, 'and just in case you didn't know it . . . .'"

Whatever professional disappointment Rigg might have felt in the aftermath of *Diana*'s demise was mitigated by the excitement she felt returning to London. Not only was the National waiting for her, but so was her new husband.

Chapter Eleven

• • • •

THE first indication that Diana may have a new romance in her life was in June 1973 when she told journalist Sydney Edwards that she was on her way to Israel, then added mysteriously, "I'm having a bit of a fling." Then, in a *Oui* magazine interview, Rigg seemingly did an about-face on her long-held public views on marriage: "I dig family. I do think it is possible to get married and stay married. But I think that's only possible if each person is prepared to improvise. It is almost impossible, without preconceived ideas about what she wants from the man or what the man wants from her or what they think they should want from each other. Oh Christ, the list of preconceived ideas is endless, really. That one should be domestically infallible; that one should be sexually receptive to; that one should be compliant; that one should be an accessory after the fact of a husband. These are the sorts of obstacles you come across, and I am not a particularly aggressive liberationist. To a large extent, I think I have got over my preconceived ideas about relationships. I am much happier now and, I think, much, much more whole than I ever was before. One trusts that, instead of going downhill, things are going to get better. I don't think I am still concerned now about what should be."

In February 1973, not long after Rigg made the break from Philip Saville, she was invited to a London dinner party. There she met Israeli artist Menahem Gueffen, who remembered their first conversation consisting of polite chatter about "Israel and her leaky roof." However, there was still enough of an attraction that Rigg volunteered to drive him home and before long, they were quietly dating. At a party to exhibit Gueffen's painting, Rigg worked the room, introducing Menahem to everyone who was anyone while wearing a revealing dress with a plunging neckline.

The relationship took a sudden turn toward permanence during a trip to Tel Aviv when Diana and Menahem got into a loud and energetic argument. Diana recalled, "We were in a hotel six floors up. I told him I was leaving. He said, 'Fine, I'll help you pack.' He did. Then he picked up my suitcase and all my clothes and threw them out of the window. I was amazed. I think it was the first time I seriously felt I had met my match."

According to *Femme Fatale* magazine, Menahem said it was a turning point in their relationship: "She became very calm, very quiet . . . and very obedient."

Diana also became convinced Menahem, who was eight years her senior and had been married twice before, was the man for her. So on the plane ride home, *she* proposed to *him*, contrary to a story run by a London paper that claimed Gueffen had demanded, "Marry me or get out!" Rigg tried to explain what impulse she was acting on: "With me, intellectual excitement is the strongest attraction next to sexual excitement. Anyone who leads me to new areas, I'm captured. This, apart from the theater and travel, is what I live for. From the beginning, I have always felt my thirty-fifth year would be the year I would inherit myself. I've always been too old for my natural years. I looked older than I was. But I knew that when I reached thirty-five it would all fit together."

Diana freely admitted that the courtship had been stormy, to say the least. At the time, it seemed that Rigg equated the arguments with unbridled passion. "We're both super-strong personalities and we will have other fights. We fight all the time, but it is a marvelous, marvelous relationship." Then Rigg joked, "I give the marriage a year." But the truth was, in the whirlwind of their engagement, any incompatibility issues were either ignored or dismissed. Diana's mom Beryl was understandably thrilled that her only daughter was finally settling down and was quick to offer practical help to move things along. Maybe she was worried Diana would change her mind or maybe she was just excited, but soon after being told of the engagement, Beryl jumped into a cab and headed for the nearest registry office. "We didn't have a clue how to go about getting married but it didn't take my mother five minutes to find out everything about the papers we needed, like Menahem's passport and all that," Diana would recall fondly years later.

In retrospect, the timing of the marriage was not ideal,

coming just one month before Rigg was scheduled to relocate to Los Angeles to film her series *Diana*. However, the
untimely demise of the sitcom meant that she and Menahem
were able to take a belated honeymoon and reacquaint themselves with one another. "We want to go to Israel to see his
country and then he wants to show me Italy. I have never
really seen Italy," she said.

In the beginning, Diana seemed committed to doing
everything possible to cement her relationship with Gueffen, including taking Jewish religious instruction. "I just
want more understanding of the faith and will take Orthodox
instruction. I want to learn and continue to learn. I have this
new relationship—my marriage—and I must learn to grow in
it. I am not totally converting," she made clear. "I'm going to
learn Hebrew. I'll read Israeli poets. Also, we want children.
Naturally, they would be brought up in their father's faith."
But when pressed on whether or not the couple was planning
to start a family right away, Diana demurred. "Babies? The
timing has to be right." Later, she was more specific to *Oui*:
"Yes, I want children but it is important that they should have
love, care and attention, and I care very much about my work.
I see the guilt of working actresses' children. Some manage,
but others are tugged dreadfully."

The couple spent a lot of time in Israel and once, on a stop-
over after attending the Tehran Film Festival, Rigg visited
wounded Israeli soldiers on the Syrian front and in the Suez.
But almost from the beginning, the marriage was strained.
First, there was the matter of Menahem's ego taking a bruising
at the perception of his being Mr. Diana Rigg. After a maga-

zine noted that Diana had enormously helped the sales of his paintings, which fetched a hefty $5,000 per canvas during a January 1974 gallery showing, by calling to attention "the fact that Miss Rigg had her spouse's price list tucked in her cleavage," Gueffen snapped to *People,* "More celebrities attended the show I staged before we'd ever met."

Menahem would also later say, "We quarreled all the time. To her, *not* quarreling was not relating." But those close to Rigg say the hot-blooded Gueffen had a violent temper that bordered on abusive. While throwing clothes out a hotel window may seem theatrically passionate during a whirlwind courtship, living with that kind of choler under the same roof is another matter altogether. The tantrums, the arguing and Menahem's alleged chair-throwing all quickly wore her patience thin, and in June 1974, just eleven months after their marriage, Diana initiated a separation.

Rigg proved to be upfront about her failed marriage and confronted the questions head-on. She told *People* in July 1974, "There is no rancor between us. I take the entire blame. I suppose it is due to my bloody awful independence. You learn something from every man in your life, be he a director or a lover. I hope my capacity to love and be loved is infinite. But I will not subscribe to anything expected of me or held socially necessary. I can be myself without being a Mrs." She would also later note: "If it hadn't been entered into in haste, it might have worked; but then if it hadn't been entered into in haste, it wouldn't have happened."

However, later she would be a little edgier when dissecting her time with Gueffen, calling it at one point a "grotesque error." In an interview with Gyles Brandreth she summed up the marriage curtly: "I contracted this mad passion and married an Israeli painter. Don't ask. It was doomed. It lasted two minutes."

Any speculation that the breakup of her marriage might rekindle her old romance with Philip Saville was quickly doused by the director himself, who told *People* magazine: "I expected her marriage to crack up. But I am genuinely sorry it has happened. When a woman has been in your life a long time, she never really leaves it. I hope to be seeing her often, but I have no plans to marry her."

Not that Diana was asking. In that same article, she said, "Quite honestly, I'd prefer living with someone. It's a greater discipline than being married, because you know you can get up and go at any time." The biggest challenge was to bounce back emotionally. "To go on living for me is to go on learning—learning about life and everything that makes life," she said. "Wanting to go on learning makes one vulnerable, of course. You are always exposing yourself to risk. I hope I can take it. I said I'd never marry but I did. I did it on impulse and that was the death knell. But I proved to people who said, 'You've never tried it,' that I tried it. I could never envisage myself staggering down that aisle again."

But simply having a physical relationship wasn't necessarily an emotional risk, because to Diana, sex and love were definitely not synonymous. "I refuse to say 'I love you' in order to legitimize the fact that I've been in bed with a fellow," she told writer Lawrence B. Eisenberg. "I don't expect him to say it to me, either. Sex is wild improvisation and shouldn't be taken too earnestly at the beginning. It is, after all, only one way of communicating—a very enjoyable one at its best—but then you get a much deeper communication, which is not necessarily commitment, but just the trust of being together continuously." Overall, Rigg noted, "The sex act is the funniest thing on the face of this earth." Which is perhaps one reason she had never bought into the sex-symbol image. "I couldn't live the life of some plastic movie queen or sex symbol," she said. "Whatever happens, I won't fall into that trap. I've always done the most ridiculous, extreme things. Whatever I do, it's because my appetite is right for it. I like to get some enjoyment out of what I'm doing. I need antidotes to relieve boredom. It appeals to me to be erratic. I think it's unfortunate that they, the critics, the audience and sometimes other actors, insist that you be consistent."

However, despite her obviously free-spirited beliefs, Diana in no way considered herself a feminist. She asserted, "Women's Lib is nonsense—so boring and unnecessary. Women have a case of discrimination but I suspect the conditioning is handed them by their mothers. So they have been their own worst enemies." She elaborated her opinion to *Cosmopolitan* in a 1973 interview: "I think what a lot of these aggressive-feminist statements lack is a sense of perspective and balance and, for God's sake, a sense of humor. They are so goddamn earnest, they drive me mad. The whole social capering that goes on between men and women and this is extremely funny. If you can't take three steps back and realize that there is a vast portion of life which is pretty droll, then you're on a treadmill. You're losing any sense of going forward, because you're trapped by your own lack of seeing something as a whole.

"Now, I'm in a business where women are given equal treatment and I'm lucky. Other women, though, have to struggle—in law, for example, or medicine—and their complaint, for the most part, is that they find it hard to get women as clients. I think the finger has to be pointed at both sexes, even as far as one's conditioning is concerned. It's not just that father came home and expected to have his dinner ready. It's also the sense you got of your mother's panic at not having his dinner ready. He probably wouldn't have shouted and screamed anyway, but those sort of fears are communicated to girl children at a very early age. I think women need to look at themselves very clearly. Given three generations of—liberated is an awful word—*aware* women, I think there'll be no problem at all, because we'll be very careful about what we communicate to our daughters."

As far as Rigg was concerned, you could be independent *and* enjoy a flirt. "I've never felt insulted when a man's admired my legs," she explained. "I don't discriminate at all. On certain occasions I have gone into an all-male milieu and discovered they were a little condescending toward me, but that didn't insult me. It quite amused me in a way because it was a defense mechanism on their part. They were not exactly sure how to deal with me."

Diana also mused on the difference in social expectations in England and America. In an interview with Michael Kustow, she recalled the reactions she got when she was working on Broadway as a single woman: "If you elect to live alone and be alone, which is what I did, with the odd escapade here, there and everywhere, then you are immediately suspect because you are predatory and socially dangerous, right? The wives don't like it. So I eventually had to take a feller around, like a handbag. He was very beautiful and not particularly bright, but he was a convenience, and I used him as such. I wouldn't dream of doing that—I wouldn't have to do it—in England. I wouldn't have to do it anywhere else in the world. But in America I did. So I thought, *'Right, I'll play that game.'*"

One game Rigg avoided during her stays in New York was playing the prima donna. "I think America is an incredibly difficult place to live in a civilized fashion," she admitted to *Oui* magazine. "And by civilized I mean ignoring the facility of everything there and creating something for yourself. In New York everyone said, 'You've got to live in an apartment block with a front door and a porter.' Bullshit. I lived in the Village and I used to walk around the streets. No problem. The Women's House of Detention was just at the end of my street and I used to walk around it as a free woman. And the women inside would look out in a fury of impotence at being locked away. They could see. Nothing could be worse, could it? At least in a prison like Dartmoor your surroundings match your situation. You look out the windows and everything is barren. But there they were, looking out the window and they could see everybody free, doing what they wanted. That's real pain and torture. Privation."

It was almost as if Rigg's theater roles continued to reflect whatever her current emotional life was at the moment. Two months after separating from Gueffen, Rigg opened in a West End revival of George Bernard Shaw's *Pygmalion*, costarring Alec McCowen as Professor Higgins. This production was much more in keeping with Shaw's original intent—that of Eliza Doolittle's growth into an independent woman no longer in need of Henry Higgins as a mentor—as director John Dexter used Shaw's first script for this staging. In the musical version of the play, *My Fair Lady*, it is clear Eliza and Higgins will end up a couple. Not so in Dexter's 1974 *Pygmalion* incarnation, and rightly so, according to Rigg. "No intelligent woman today would accept that ending—not Eliza going back to being a doormat and being insulted," she said. "Eliza is equipped for a life by herself."

Dexter added, "I rather agree with the critic who said Eliza would go out and do something for women's suffrage."

A comment written by Shaw in the epilogue of *Pygmalion* seems to validate Rigg and Dexter: "Eliza, in telling Higgins she would not marry him if he asked, was not coquetting: she was announcing a well-considered decision. . . . She will marry him because she must marry anybody who will provide for her. But at Eliza's age a good-looking girl does not feel that pressure: she feels free to pick and choose. She is therefore guided by her instinct in the matter. Eliza's instinct tells her not to marry Higgins. . . . When Higgins excused his indifference to young women on the ground that they had an irresistible rival in his mother, he gave the clue to his inveterate old-bachelordom."

While *My Fair Lady* was cinematic spun sugar, Dexter's *Pygmalion* was often raw. A review in the *Los Angeles Times* notes: "When this Eliza and Professor Higgins return from their ultimate triumph at Buckingham Palace, she doesn't float about in rapture over how she could have danced all night. She throws his slippers in his face, they have a slamming row and she walks out." The review goes on to say that the heart and soul of the production is Rigg's performance. "The core of Dexter's near-perfect production is Diana Rigg's Eliza—unbending, accepting any humiliation necessary to make her a lady, but pliant only so far. Its heart is its uncompromising ending—Eliza refusing to be overwhelmed, growing into an immovable object capable of meeting McCowen's irresistible force.

"*Pygmalion* always had style and wit and a lot of home truths. Now, it also has power."

Ironically, for all the kudos showered upon her for her dramatic work, Diana admitted to theater writer Marilyn Stasio that she had a special fondness for comedy roles: "I think that dramatic roles, not just Lady Macbeth, can give you a sort of quiet satisfaction if you think it's been strong. But comedy really makes you feel you can go on to the goodies afterwards. That's true whether it's Emma Peel or Adrianna or anything. You *flow*, you're much more *liquid*, so you're really beautiful. Comedy's a beginning; Lady Macbeth is an ending."

But regardless of the role onstage, one's social life during a major run is practically nonexistent. As Diana put it, "It's impossible to do anything. In the theater, they do work you incredibly hard. You lead a pretty disciplined life because you have only so much energy and you have to conserve it. You have a 10:30 A.M. rehearsal, followed by an evening performance."

Despite the single-mindedness of theater work, Rigg still vastly preferred it to film work. "It's nicer, I suppose because in the end you are responsible for what you do. Nobody can muck about with it. If anybody's going to fail, it's going to be you. You don't have someone making you up. You make yourself up; you get yourself together; you go onstage. You're responsible for your movements all the time. You don't have a second assistant hovering around waiting for you. You've been to film studios; you know how revoltingly they treat you. They don't mean to but they just think you are totally irresponsible because you're an actress. You *can* make too many bad movies or too many dull TV shows," she affirmed to *After Dark*, "but in the theater, the more you work the better it is."

However, television and film work were necessary aspects of her career, if for no other reason than to pay the bills. "I have a contract with the National which allows for eight or nine months in and eight or nine months out," Rigg explained. "It's a very realistic arrangement because you don't make much money at the National." But Diana was often disappointed in the scripts she was offered: "I don't think they're very good, generally speaking. They lack truth, a view of things which is specific yet fresh, the difference between truth and something which comes tripping off the tongue. Really, I am not good in movies; my face is too wide and I am altogether too big in that." It was also an annoyance that in her experience, many producers equated "seriousness with dowdiness." As Rigg put it, "I don't see why sex and intellect have to be self-defeating."

As a result, Rigg tended to gravitate more toward small-screen projects. So after productions of *Phaedra Brittanica* and *The Misanthrope* at the National, Rigg filmed a made-for-TV movie of *In This House of Brede*. Adapted by James Costigan from the best-selling novel by Rumer Godden, the movie stars Rigg as a widowed, successful business executive named Philippa Talbott in search of a more meaningful life. To the shock of her friends, and dismay of her boyfriend, Philippa enters a cloistered order of Benedictine nuns at Brede Abbey. The movie aired on CBS as a GE Theater TV special in February 1975.

For some, the idea of the outspoken Rigg playing a cloistered nun seems an unusual choice, perhaps because the typical perception of nuns tends to be of religious nonentities with no particular individualism. But Rigg disagreed it was a professional non sequitur. "I see nothing unusual in me playing a nun," she said. "Nuns can be very humorous and very realistic. They don't meld into one personality. I knew one, the head of a library, who knew all about life through books. We discussed *Edwardians in Love* in terms of its sensuality." For her performance, Diana was nominated for an Outstanding Lead Actress in a Special Program Emmy, but lost out to fellow Brit Juliet Mills' turn in *QB VII*.

While filming the TV movie, which shot on location in real Irish and English abbeys, Rigg was also in rehearsals for reprising her role in *The Misanthrope*, which was opening on Broadway at the St. James in March 1975. In Molière's play, Alceste, the misanthrope, refuses to participate in society's insincerities and mindless civilities. He is honest to a fault and that inability to cushion his feelings alienates him from most people. Ironically, the one person he isn't honest with is himself, in that he can't accept that the world is not such a black-and-white universe. On the other hand, Célimène, the young woman he is attracted to, plays fast and loose with honesty and is more concerned about maintaining a suitable number of suitors. The production reunited Diana with old friends Alec McCowen, who would be her costar, and director John Dexter. However, as she told the *New York Times*, this production would be a different animal than the one that was staged in London two years earlier.

"I can't simply do a Lazarus act, you know, treading along the same lines I did in 1973. It has to have some new meaning for me now. I once thought of Célimène as one whose path was flower-strewn, sunlit, perfumed. Now I'm finding her slightly more difficult, possibly because what satisfied me two years ago doesn't satisfy me now. Célimène has dark shades, yes, but they're heavily disguised under a veneer of lightness and sophistication. And she's a fluid woman, very sexual, incapable of deep commitment, afraid of being alone. There are aspects of her in every woman. It's easy to lend one's heart, to get on that whirlwind of sexual and social promises, to move for the sake of moving, without thinking," she explained. Diana had such a specific take on Célimène that she had a hand in the wardrobe, instructing her costume designer the character should "be wearing golden browns and creams, never any underwear." She added, "Her body has to be evident, fluid—nothing stiff to imprison her personality."

Put bluntly, Rigg explained in a *Cue* interview, Célimène

"is a bitch—a witty bitch, but a bitch." She continued, "She's terribly sexual, of course; she'll do anything just to keep a circle of panting males around her. That's because she feels empty by herself, without people around her. She's a young woman who is so frantically avoiding loneliness that she must be all things to all men in order to be constantly surrounded by people; in order, you see, not ever to be left alone with herself."

"I do adore playing the part," Rigg said, throwing off the illusion. "She brings out all the things which I dislike in women, and which I try to avoid doing in my own life. You know— that calculated seductiveness, that partial commitment some women make to men, just to keep them around, waiting."

When Molière wrote the play, he set it in the royal courts of 1600s France, but Dexter and writer Tony Harrison contemporized it and set it three hundred years later, in Charles de Gaulle's 1966 Paris. "Harrison is a scholar and a poet, and he therefore avoids that perversity of doing things just because they're *in*," Rigg told writer Marilyn Stasio. "There always have to be reasons, beyond the appetite of the director, for taking plays out of their periods and putting them in other periods. Often it's done just because it looks pretty." But in this case, Diana explained, "there were obvious correlations between the two periods. De Gaulle was like the court kings of the seventeenth century, and not merely in terms of his power and influence. He created the atmosphere of a kingly court, partially restoring the monarchy and its rigid social structure. This, of course, led to that sycophancy among his followers, which is what Molière's play is all about."

Rigg continued, commenting on the centuries-old rift between England and France. "French society hasn't changed all that much since 1666," she said. "There is still that incredible snobbery, which is why one should never feel paranoid when one visits France. It's absolutely true that the French don't like foreigners; they dislike themselves heartily, so why should you be any exception to their dislike?"

But, that said, Diana acknowledged that her own homeland also had its share of issues: "We have a monarchy ourselves, so it was easy to draw parallels. It's not as rigid as one might think, but you know very well if you're *in* or *out*. The upper classes can be as rude or as obscene as they wish—about their lineage and their natural speaking of style—but they are always rude or obscene with *style*."

When *The Misanthrope* opened, Rigg once again became the toast of the theatrical town. Henry Hewes of the *Saturday Review* wrote: "For proof of how a classic repertory system can expand the talent of performers, one only has to look at Diana Rigg in the National Theater production of *The Misanthrope*, currently visiting Broadway. Ms. Rigg began her career as a pretty ingénue whose promise was no greater than that of a dozen others her age. She turned to television and became popular in a series called *The Avengers*. Then she turned her back on the big money to join the National and gain the chance to tackle roles that demanded all her intelligence and that forced her to acquire new skills. . . .

"Ms. Rigg shows up this tragedy every twinkling step of the way, and she is generously assisted by Alec McCowen, who plays Alceste as an outrageously impossible Puritan.

When Célimène turns down the proposal to marry him and live far away from Paris, Ms. Rigg is devastating as she wisely tells him, 'I'm only twenty! I'd be terrified! Just you and me and all that countryside!' Her final moment alone among the elegant ruins is utterly poignant, a triumph for her and all ingénues who would be actresses."

Cue's Marilyn Stasio said: "Diana Rigg is Célimène to the (bared) teeth. Her wicked triumph is in seducing Alceste, and us, into adoring all her brilliant artifice, even as we see clearly into her petty little soul."

Diana seemed to appreciate the U.S. reviews in a different way from when critics in England lavished her with praise. "The critics back home are always saying that I'm *growing* or *stretching*," she observed. "God knows what they mean by that. I suspect that the critical establishment has simply never forgiven me for doing *The Avengers,* and this is their way of welcoming me back to respectability. But English actors are not afraid to do something trashy, for whatever reason."

Her performance in *The Misanthrope* earned Rigg her second "Best Actress in a Play" Tony nomination. And for the second time, she failed to take the statue home. But while Ellen Burstyn won the Tony for *Same Time, Next Year,* Diana didn't come away empty-handed. She made a bet with a friend that if she won, she would take him to dinner; if she lost, he would spring for the bill. The catch was, the restaurant could be anywhere in the world. After losing, Rigg said she consoled herself trying to find "the most exotic restaurant in the farthest place in the world." As she explained, "Yes, he has to pay for transportation and everything. I think I'll choose someplace in the Far East."

But *The Misanthrope* would turn out to be Rigg's last professional triumph for a while. Over the following decade, Diana would take on a new role that would consume her in a way no theater production ever had—that of mother.

Chapter Twelve

• • • •

ALTHOUGH she wouldn't actually divorce Menahem Gueffen until 1976, as soon as Diana filed for separation she was spiritually and emotionally a single woman again. If she grieved over the loss of the relationship, she did so out of the public's eye. Instead, what pervaded Rigg's conversations was more an aftertaste of disappointment, resignation—and hope. Despite the marriage not working out, Diana refused to put up any walls, of either bitterness or sentimentality, and still viewed relationships with clear-eyed candor and openness. She once observed that she didn't have a definite idea of the type of man she was predominantly attracted to in a physical sense. "It changes," she explained. "I don't ever have one fixed idea. They've all been completely different, thank God. I used to hate redheaded men until I had a redheaded lover and I was really turned on by redheads for a long time. It's just whatever's going."

However, culturally it was a different story. During an

appearance on *The Tonight Show* she told Johnny Carson that she thought "American men are boring companions and bad lovers." She clarified her sentiments later to writer Michael T. Leech: "That was an abrasive statement and obviously a generalization. Besides, it sounded as if I'd had just about everything in sight to make such a statement, which, of course, isn't true. I *do* find the sexual aspect of life really not too good in America. There are certain priorities here, which I think have nothing to do with what sex is about. Americans seem to want to bundle everything into the sex act and you can't do that. American men drag an emotional content into lovemaking, which you don't need, unless it's truly, honestly there. You don't just make love and then suddenly love someone. There are these women saying, 'Now do you love me?' or, 'Do you love me still?' and they are confused. . . .

"Sex and love have to be separated. They *have* to be. There is a carnal element in sex. You needn't be guilty about that. Neither need you make excuses because your body needs it. You can make love with a man and not see him again until a cocktail party three weeks later. There's nothing wrong with that, the fact that you haven't lived in each others' pockets for the previous three weeks. You have to be realistic and say, 'I enjoyed it but obviously he didn't because he hasn't called back.' So then you say *tant pis*, it's just one of those things. How many people do you meet socially that you really want to see again?"

At thirty-six years old, Diana had firmly established herself as one of Britain's top stage actresses. As such, like all public figures, she was regularly contacted by organizations and individuals looking for her to either use her celebrity to champion their cause or to make a cash donation. But for

Rigg, any charitable contribution or personal involvement to a cause had to come from the heart. "I must be committed. I must feel for a protest before I'll do anything," she said in an *After Dark* interview. "I do feel very much for the liberation of women, but I think it's a very individual effort rather than a mass movement, although I naturally agree with the principles of equal pay, equal opportunities, etcetera. The mass movement is helpful in bringing people together, perhaps also in publicizing its causes, but I do believe that the real battle must be fought alone—by yourself, for your own values, and for your own freedom. Freedom is a word that's used far too easily nowadays, because I think it's a very hard thing and also a very personal thing to achieve."

Sometimes, the solicitations Rigg received seemed surreal. "I've had requests to help save Venice," she said. "It was explained pigeons cause a great deal of damage to the buildings of Venice and a birth control pill for pigeons had now been developed. They wanted to raise £40,000 to buy supplies of the pill to put among the pigeons. It was so bizarre I nearly accepted." Ironically, even though Rigg was now in a financial position to donate money, she still had a hard time lavishing it on herself, a trait she believed was a direct result of her Yorkshire upbringing. "I never had much—we never had much as a family—so when I buy anything for myself I am disturbed by it. I don't take it out of its wrappings for up to a week. It is pure guilt," she said.

Then, perhaps when she was least expecting it, Rigg found herself falling in love with a man she could actually envision spending the rest of her life with. In 1975, Diana attended a dinner party where she met wealthy businessman Archibald Hugh Stirling, a former Guards officer and Scottish laird who also dabbled in producing. Stirling was the dashing son of a founding member of the SAS regiments of World War II and swept Rigg away, despite the fact that he was married. A year after Diana's divorce from Gueffen became final, she gave birth to her and Archie's daughter, Rachael Atlanta, in May 1977. Suddenly everything was different, and for the first time in her adult life, theater wasn't Diana's primary passion. Now, her daughter and life with Archie was. But unlike Philip Saville, Archie Stirling divorced his wife to be with Diana.

"Before that there was nothing to stop me or give me pause," Rigg told *TV Guide*'s Sharon Rosenthal. "I would grab a holiday between jobs, and if I wasn't working on something, I'd be preparing for something. And I loved every minute of it. But I had worked solidly for eighteen years and, by that time, I had become aware that the career just wasn't going to be enough. Pregnancy, and all that came with it, was enjoyable, relaxing. The comparative quiet in one's life that follows having a baby . . . this is another kind of happiness, which I suppose in the end is more long-lasting, although, I don't know. I rather think it's in the nature of my personality that I have a sort of a single-minded streak." All the energy she had previously put into her career had to share space with Rachael and Archie. She explained: "You know, it's absolutely hellish working with a child and family miles away. It's hellish. I don't know how other people do it; I'm just deeply divided and unhappy being away. So what's the point?"

Happily for Diana, her mom lived to see Rachael born.

But in 1980, Beryl died, leaving a bereft Rigg behind. "My mother died in a heart operation," she said. "I went to bed for three days and just stared at the ceiling, feeling grief and guilt—'*Had I done enough? Should I have allowed the operation to go ahead?*'—and all that baggage, all that adolescent rebellion to feel guilty about." Nine years earlier, Rigg's dad, Louis, had succumbed to cancer, so now she was no longer anybody's child. But Diana was aware that her mother's final years without Louis had been difficult. "My mother was just marking time after my father went," Rigg told Gyles Brandreth. "She was very much of that generation whose life was her husband. I wonder if women nowadays are going to be quite as bereft when their husbands die. I don't think so." Thinking back to her father's death, Diana said, "I loved him, very deeply. Though I probably never really let him know."

For several years after Rachael's birth, Rigg went on a professional hiatus. Then, when Rachael was four years old, Rigg began taking the occasional acting job. One of the jobs she took seemed to be a direct reaction to being a parent. In 1981 she costarred in *The Great Muppet Caper* which, she says, "impressed Rachael tremendously." In the film, Kermit and Fozzie are intrepid reporters who go to London on the trail of an international jewelry thief who has stolen a priceless diamond necklace from Lady Holiday, a wealthy fashion designer. While there, Kermit falls in love with Holiday's secretary, Miss Piggy. "I portrayed Lady Holiday—where her title comes from I'm not exactly sure," Rigg says. "I suppose she was born into the gentry or she married a lord. In terms of my characterization I suspect it was the latter; I don't really think she's on her own running one of London's most elegant fashion houses. She's sort of Coco Chanel three times larger, very flamboyant and rather overpowering. No wonder Miss Piggy desperately wants to be a Holiday Model!"

Rigg joked that despite her history of martial-arts moves, Miss Piggy was one high-kicking adversary she would rather not face. "Alas, I have no scenes with Miss Piggy where we go into karate," Rigg said during a press interview. "However, I don't think she needs any tuition in that direction. She's got her own method. It's not really karate or kung fu. It's something very special to Miss Piggy."

Working with her Muppet costars was an exhilarating, and unique, experience for Diana. She explained, "What has been so marvelous about doing this movie is that I have not had any other experience like it. I seem to have spent most of my career doing things I have never done before. And I absolutely adore the Muppets. I've watched all their programs on television and in fact we taped them for Rachael. We have a half hour every night before she goes to sleep which is totally devoted to Muppets. We both love each and every one of those magical little characters. It's lovely to have something like that to share with Rachael."

Her next roles were a little less kid-friendly. In late 1981, she appeared in *Evil Under the Sun*, a film adaptation of Agatha Christie's novel, then made her return to the Broadway stage in a musical called *Colette*, based on the life of the famed French writer. The music was composed by Harvey Schmidt, and Tom Jones wrote the text and lyrics—the same team that had written *The Fantasticks*. Originally, Debbie

Reynolds had been cast as the lead but backed out after she accepted a role in the TV series *Aloha Paradise*, a spin-off of *The Love Boat*. *Colette*'s producer, Harry Rigby, was philosophical: "Let's face it; everybody needs money." As long as there were changes afoot, the producer also replaced the original director, Frank Dunlop. "I don't know how to be tactful about it—it just didn't work out," Rigby said. However, in retrospect, the early turmoil simply set the stage for the disaster to follow.

For years Rigg had wanted to do a musical. So even though it meant relocating to America, she agreed to step in, although she admitted, "I have no idea how I was offered the role," considering her lack of musical experience. Diana described Colette as "someone who broke ground and made a stand for independence." She went on to explain, "I was

Rigg and the chorus from the musical *Colette*

in New York for three days to hear the music for the show and was delighted. I don't wish to be derogatory about English musicals—that's not my bag—but American musicals are brilliantly done. If you are going to do a musical, you want to learn from the very best people."

The plan was to rehearse in New York, then take the musical on a five-city west coast tour as a tune-up for its Broadway debut. Not only was starring as the lead in a big-budget, splashy American musical a career first for Rigg, so was the experience of dealing with a furry, four-legged costar. Colette was famous for her love of cats, so in the musical, several scenes call for a cat to be onstage as a warm-blooded prop. However, while on tour in Denver, the cat bit Rigg and inflicted a rather serious wound, after which Diana demanded the cat be "sacked." So an eight-year-old replacement cat named Fuzzy was hired. One of the selling points was that Fuzzy was declawed. And just in case Fuzzy had a sudden surge of rage, the producers also hired two understudy felines—Mr. Boots and Daffy.

Local newspapers had fun running stories about the cat casting call. Unfortunately, though, critics didn't find the musical nearly as entertaining. *Colette* opened in Seattle to terrible reviews. Not even Rigg's baring her breasts in an Egyptian costume scene could add any zing, or interest, to the lackluster staging. Producer Rigby responded by commenting, "There are a lot of good restaurants in Seattle, and all that rain is good for complexions and plants—but not for shows."

But after an equally tepid reception in Denver, producers

abruptly pulled the plug on the tour, announcing they were taking it back to New York for "retooling" and a new round of rehearsals. It was also announced there would be a new director, a new set designer and new choreography—in short, basically a new play. It was a brave front, but in the following week came the inevitable report that the show would not go on. Instead, the producers decided to take an extended break for extended rewrites, meaning that Rigg was no longer contractually committed to the show and that the producers had lost a $1.5 million investment.

Later, Diana would accept responsibility for the fiasco, claiming her performance was seriously lacking. "I don't consider myself a *singer*; I am somebody who interprets songs," she said. "I don't mean that to sound very grand. I have to say that because I don't make the beautiful sounds that singers make."

While *Colette*'s demise in March of 1982 might have been a humbling professional experience, Rigg would remember that time for quite another reason. Whether it was because she longed for a marriage like her parents had shared or that she felt assured that her relationship with Stirling was indeed for the long haul, after five years of togetherness, Rigg and Archie were married on March 25 at City Hall in New York City, with then-city clerk and future mayor David Dinkins performing the ceremony. Rigg admitted that this time around, the experience of marriage was very different than with Gueffen. Specifically, she was surprised at "how exciting it was, how romantic it was, how it deepened everything." She said, "I believed it was a relationship to last."

The experience of *Colette* also convinced Diana it was time for a change in lifestyle. During her time in America, she had brought Rachael with her. "The poor little sprogget was in one nursery school then another," Rigg explained. "I realized it was impossible, that I wasn't going to subject her to this. That she had a right to have—every child has a right—to a secure home. So that meant good-bye to anymore work in America until my daughter was of an age when she could travel with me or when she would be away at boarding school, not much before she's twelve or thirteen. It meant choosing very carefully what I did so that it didn't bite into the school holidays. So I could be there at the school gates to pick her up." When she did work, Diana recalled to Matt Wolf, "We'd do a little bargaining: if I did a job, I then promised not to work again. So every time I went to work, Rachael knew there'd be a period when it would all stop and I'd be back home."

Back in Scotland, Diana made the transition to marital domesticity with seeming ease. The former workaholic was now a grand lady of the manor. She and Archie split their time between their London home in Kensington and Stirling's family estate in Perthshire, Scotland, where Archie farmed 5,000 acres. Rigg doted on her daughter, fished and became more deeply involved in religion, the latter an outgrowth of having a child.

The disappointment of *Colette* was no doubt easier to digest because of Rigg's happiness with her home life. Back in Scotland, Diana said she and Archie enjoyed walks, picnics and the fresh air. "Up there I am my husband's wife," she explained. The woman who had lived her life being unconventional had finally settled down, but it wasn't being married that had caused the change. "No, not with marriage—with a child, I became conventional," Diana told Grace Bradberry. "I backpedaled my career because I wanted to be consistent, yes? If it were said that I didn't fulfill my potential as a mother and a wife I'd be heartbroken. But if it were said I hadn't achieved my full potential as an actress, I would understand the reasons why. And I discovered I had a religion which I hadn't been brought up with. Out of you is coming this other being which is going to develop. I had a good assessment of what I was and had been, and I had an ambition of the kind of mother that I wanted to be. I wanted to give her a really safe base, where I could share with her my beliefs." However, she admitted her beliefs were "creaky prayers to begin with." She explained, "And then, when Rachael was born, she was christened, and when she got older, I wrote a prayer for her to say when I was putting her to bed. In a church, I get great joy and stimulation." Rigg attended church faithfully and enrolled her daughter in a Sunday school.

Because Diana was so determined that Rachael have the freedom to be an individual, she was not amused when others made assumptions, such as the ones made the time Rachael was cast in a school play. Diana explains: "Rachel got a good part and I rather resented that because one of the delights of children is that they are different. And there were these people who were pushing her into being a little version of me. But I didn't say anything, because she was thrilled to play those parts."

Despite her father's heritage and her mother's fame,

Rachael bristles at the suggestion her childhood was posh. "It wasn't a Jane Austen-esque childhood," she says. "Yes, the house was beautiful, but it wasn't a castle. It didn't have, you know, wings." Stirling describes herself growing up as "a complete nightmare, I'm sure—energetic, always riding my pony and swimming in rivers—and pretty self-contained." She goes on to explain, "There weren't any kids living next door. I didn't go to balls. . . . Okay, I went to one, called the Northern Meeting, but no one filled in my dance card. No dashing white sergeant whisked me off my feet. I was a big, big lass, you see. I didn't start to feel remotely attractive until I was twenty-one."

All the time spent outside nurtured a deep love of the land in Rachael, and she considers Scotland, not England, her homeland. "This is going to sound a bit slushy," she says, "but I feel like Vivien Leigh in *Gone With the Wind* about it. I've got to go there, just to touch the earth. And every time I come back down south, England just seems so small and petty. Scotland's got this vastness, those huge hills where nobody is ever going to build a suburb."

Although Rigg may not have been treading the boards much, theater remained very much a part of her. In 1982, she edited a book called *No Turn Unstoned: The Worst Ever Theatrical Reviews*, a compilation of three hundred critical pans inspired in part by John Simon's snarky review of Rigg in *Abelard and Heloise*. "The book started over a long and rather boozy dinner," Diana recalled. "We were a mixed group of actors, directors and musicians, and in the course of the evening the talk turned to bad notices. We were able to laugh over something that had

© HULTON-DEUTSCH COLLECTION/CORBIS

Helen Mirren as Cassandra and Diana Rigg as Kytemnestra in a scene from the 1979 BBC production of *The Serpent Son*, based on Aeschylus' Greek tragedy *The Oresteia*

deeply hurt us. It proved cathartic. I decided then to write the book in the belief that no matter how great or grand, everyone must some time in their career have had one; there is bound to be a bad choice of play or misconceived performance."

Diana first collected the reviews from acting colleagues in Britain, as well as reviews of some deceased actors "who have gone on eternal tour." She then contacted peers in America and was surprised at the number of people who refused to participate. "The famous and secure wrote back—Hepburn, Heston, Bacall," she said. "But to a disappointing number of people, failure was a rude word. One actress wrote back and said she'd had a lobotomy and couldn't remember her bad notices!"

For Rigg, the book was as uplifting as it was amusing. "I

consider this book to be about how every one of us has failed, and survived," she said. "You learn much more from your failures than you do from your successes. And a lot of failures are terribly funny. Every time you quote your own bad notice you exorcise a little of the pain. The book is not just an actor's way of getting back at a critic. After you've spent a night of boredom, the temptation to pan must be very great."

Working on the book prompted Rigg to research the history of critical writing and she found the subject so fascinating, she gave an impromptu lecture on it during a visit to the Library of Congress in 1992. "I learned in my research that critical writing was not considered a profession until the eighteenth century," she explained. Prior to that, it was left to historians to immortalize performers. She went on: "I find it a comfort to read about actors in the seventeenth century forgetting their lines. We still do it. I find it fascinating that hundreds of years ago society found aspects of the theater disturbing. But you, the audience, have a right to criticize what you see. Bad notices go as far back as the earliest known actor, Thespus.

"He founded our profession and received the first bad notice doing it during the course of a play around 560 B.C." In this play, Thespus broke character to impersonate a god. "Ambitious actors are famous for improving their parts," Diana deadpanned. Despite acting's public appeal, the keepers of society had mixed feelings about the profession. "Plato would have exiled the acting profession in his ideal Republic," Rigg noted, describing what happened after Thespus won the top prize in an Athens acting competition. "He wrote: 'In our state, such as he are not permitted to exist. The law will not allow them. So after we have anointed him with myrrh, we shall send him away to another city.'" Rigg paused, then added, "The first instance of 'Don't call us; we'll call you.'"

She also noted that criticism took a more ominous tone with the emergence of the Catholic Church: "Up to this time the critics had pretty much confined themselves to saying, 'I don't approve.' Now they'd begun to declare with mounting conviction that 'God doesn't approve!'" Through it all, she says, "We do survive. Actors have come a long way since Thespus."

Rigg returned to television in the 1987 made-for-TV movie *A Hazard of Hearts*. Based on a Barbara Cartland romance novel, the period piece is set in early nineteenth-century England and tells the story of the beautiful Serena, whose compulsive-gambler father, Sir Giles Staverly, wagers his daughter's hand in marriage in a dice game. He loses. Rather than have to face Serena and tell her she is now betrothed to the evil Lord Wrotham, he commits suicide. Feeling pity for a girl he never met, Lord Vulcan, who witnessed the events, challenges Lord Wrotham to a double-or-nothing bet. Vulcan wins both Serena's hand *and* the Staverly family home but has no intention of collecting on the bet, until he meets the beautiful Serena.

Marking a definite transition in her career, Diana was cast as Lord Vulcan's mother. While some actresses lament leaving their ingénue days behind, Rigg, now forty-nine, seemed to take it in stride and chose to view it as just another professional challenge. "I've always done different things," she explained. "I've got quixotic tastes. There is a specific style about period pieces that you must find and reach. It is a mixture of what would be two centuries ago plus a bit of modernism. But you must be real, you can't be cardboard. At the same time it is telling a story that is old-fashioned, but you *must* make it entertaining. The same overriding disciplines always remain the same. If you are playing that type of lady you must have authority, a straight back and terrific diction."

Despite her comfort playing the Gothic maternal figure, Rigg wasn't quite ready to relinquish her leading-lady status. "I'm not a character actress yet," she told *People* in 1986. "If I'm clever about what parts I play, I'll stay a leading lady for fifteen years. Then I'll switch to character roles." However, she did acknowledge that she was now past the age of the great female Shakespearean roles: "Shakespeare is my favorite, but as you get older the parts for women get duller." Still, even a dulled Shakespearean role was something to treasure. As Diana explained, "Each time you perform a Shakespearean role there are shades to be discovered, which is what makes them fascinating for actors and audiences. You can see one actor do one interpretation of a role and see another do the same role and they can be different but equally viable. I think that is what makes them extraordinary and, in the end, challenging."

However, Rigg also dreamed of starring in a play written specifically for her: "That is the greatest gift of all because it means somebody knows you and enjoys your work and is therefore going to write for the parts of you that are the best. It has never happened, but I would like it to."

Also in 1987, Rigg got back on the musical horse by appearing in a London revival of Stephen Sondheim's *Follies*. The musical, originally staged in 1972 and the winner of a Tony for Best Musical, is considered to be one of Sondheim's best. The plot revolves around a reunion of middle-aged former Follies girls to commemorate the soon-to-be-demolished Weisman Theater in New York. Unlike the music of *Colette*, Sondheim's lyrics are less dependent on tonal ability than they are on interpretation, so in this environment, Rigg flourished as the character of Phyllis, the role Alexis Smith had won the Tony for on Broadway in the original company.

"They are just the toughest things of all," Rigg said of musicals. "The energy level is something phenomenal. And then there is the discipline of the orchestration, and having to come in on exactly the right half-beat or whatever. Singing a song is like being on the London to Edinburgh express. If you want to get off at York, forget it." But *Follies* was an exhilarating experience. "I had not done a musical of this kind before," Rigg explained, "and I had never tap-danced onstage—that was a challenge. It is a wonderful part, and the songs I sing do not require a trained voice. I couldn't tell you what I will do after *Follies* but I suspect it will be something far removed from tap-dancing on the musical stage."

Was it ever. Rigg apparently decided that if she was now bound to play her share of maternal roles, she would do so with a vengeance. And in the process, she would have critics falling all over themselves trying to come up with appropriate adjectives to laud her performance.

In the miniseries *Mother Love*, Rigg plays Helena Vesey, a homicidally vindictive woman who is obsessed with her son Kit. She resents his new wife and the happiness Kit has found with her even more than she resents her ex-husband's happiness with *his* American wife and their family. The more Helena is engulfed with a burning madness and a need for revenge against her son and ex-spouse, the closer she is pushed to murder. The movie was based on the thriller of the same name written by British author Roger Longrigg under the pseudonym Domini Taylor.

When it came time to cast the lead role, producer Ken Riddington and director Simon Langton each wrote down a wish list, and when they compared, Diana was at the top of both their lists. But when they first approached her, Rigg initially found it beyond believability that anyone could be as over-the-top as Helena. So to convince her, the producer had a psychiatrist review the script. The doctor thought Helena was believable, especially among women who feel their families slipping away. "I read the psychiatrist's report," Diana recalled to Deborah Ross. "I needed to know, 'Why?' And it explained she has been rejected by her mother and therefore never grew up. Although Helena has a child, that child is an extension of her. She lives vicariously through her son.

"She's so tight and tidy and neat—that represents how repressed she is. She never liked sex, not for an instant. She wanted the family unit, but she didn't want to go to bed with her husband. She sees herself as a sort of Joan of Arc, a righter of wrongs. When she murders her former husband's second wife, she does not think she's done anything horrific. It's justice.

"I had to keep asking the director to stop me if I was

going over the top. I had to measure out the degree of madness because it accelerated with every episode. It is a bit like running a marathon—you have to pace yourself until you get into the stadium and run the final distance. That's how I played Helena."

Although she relished the chance to inhabit such a character, Rigg qualified it by saying, "You can't be *attracted* to Helena. It's just a role you can't turn down. A villainess is far more interesting than a villain. A male villain may wreak more physical damage, but a woman villain has more depth. She has to be subtler, psychologically more labyrinthine, than he is. If you start with a good fairy at the cradle, you don't have much of a story.

"I took the role because it is a very good part and I suppose it was a slight departure from the roles I have played over the years. I just knew I would enjoy doing it and I think that is the criteria you have to apply, because in the end if you enjoy doing it, it comes across to the audience."

Beyond the psychiatrist's report, Rigg had to gain a sense of Helena in her gut. "We make a quantum leap in my business between what you know and what your instinct tells you of people," she explained to Sandra McLean. "If you have never met anybody like that, with the same manic qualities going on inside you, you have to use your imagination, and this is what one does when you play a character who is very far removed from yourself. I think it is easier for an actor to be extreme, but credibility was a large consideration in this case. One had to be believed, otherwise it would just spin off into melodrama, and I mean *mel*odrama. It's very difficult to show the duality in her—her insanity and her outward appearance. You have to show only the tip of the iceberg. So I had to discipline myself, because I am vaguely irreverent anyway and tend to see the funny side. There is a touch of very subtle pastiche in the whole thing, which those who relish this will see." Tapping into Helena's madness was perhaps a bit *too* easy. "I wasn't thinking of anything specific or calling up memories, but I was horrified by how much I could find there," Rigg admitted.

Diana was also bemused by some of the reaction she got on the street. She recalls, "A woman in a supermarket came up to me and it was remarkable. She told me how terribly I was behaving and how much she was enjoying it." Actually the most remarkable thing about that anecdote is that Rigg still grocery shopped for herself rather than have some personal assistant schlepping for her, as would be the case with most American actresses of her stature.

Ironically, when *Mother Love* aired on PBS' long-running *Mystery!* series, Rigg had the surreal task of introducing herself. In the autumn of 1989, she took over as the show's host for her longtime friend Vincent Price after he announced his retirement. Although the series gave her weekly exposure on American TV, the intros to the episodes were shot during two brief trips a year to Boston—a schedule that fit nicely with her self-imposed work restrictions. While Vincent Price might have seemed a natural choice for hosting a mystery anthology, Rigg was picked for her, well, Britishness, as all the shows were U.K. imports.

"I'm not a great mystery reader myself," Rigg admitted,

"but I think that mystery stories translate beautifully to television, and I have always watched them with real enjoyment. So, you would be correct in calling me a fan. I also think that mysteries are done incredibly well and with great style on British television."

In interviews she conducted to promote *Mystery!*, everything in Diana's life seemed practically idyllic. Her biggest trauma seemed to be adjusting to then-twelve-year-old Rachael leaving home to attend the Wycombe Abbey boarding school. "Oh, yes, that was traumatic for both mother and daughter," Diana admitted to James Brady. "I'm on the phone to her every day." Despite not having a child at home full time, Rigg still had no interest in seeking out any work on Broadway. "I wouldn't commit to a year's run until she's standing on her own two feet," she declared.

With Rachael away at school, it would have seemed a perfect opportunity for Diana and Archie to have more time to enjoy one another, but the public image of their perfect marriage proved to be an illusion. On Valentine's Day in 1990, Archie was spotted having a romantic dinner, but not with Diana. Stirling had begun an affair with Joely Richardson, the twenty-five-year-old daughter of Vanessa Redgrave and apparently no longer cared who knew. It was a case of the wife being the last to know. Rigg learned of the affair only after friends complimented her on being so courageous about it. When Stirling announced he was leaving, Diana did not take the news well; her immediate reaction was to clear his closets of clothes and ship them off to charity. Although Archie eventually broke off the affair with Richardson and returned to

Diana in hopes of salvaging their marriage, the damage was done, and his attempt at reconciliation failed. In September 1990, Rigg filed for divorce. It was a stunningly abrupt end to what had been one of Britain's fairy-tale marriages.

The pain of a relationship disintegrating is something most people have experienced and can empathize with. But knowing that strangers on the street know the intimate details of your loss and failure is something that can only be understood by those who live in the public eye. Rigg refused to show any public weakness. "I'm not going to play the grieving divorcée with a tear-stained face," she said to Jeremy Watson. "It's not a particularly good part; it has lousy lines and absolutely no laughs. It's also a very boring role to play."

However, she would later reveal in the *Daily Mail* that she mourned the loss of her marriage for a long time. She explained, "In public I bounced back. I took on the greatest roles I'd ever had. But in private I was grieving about the passing of something I valued so deeply. But the best thing a woman can do is acknowledge that it is over and move on." Although she was seen as the wronged woman, Rigg refused to use her celebrity as a podium to dress Stirling down. He was, after all, still the father of the daughter she adored. Plus, it simply wasn't in Rigg to play the victim. "I take fifty percent of the blame for what happened," she said. "I feel much better if I do that."

The tabloids couldn't get enough of the breakup, reporting it in screaming headlines and breathless revelations. Rigg, who had always been accessible and candid to the media, felt betrayed, particularly by female British tabloid journalists who she started referring to as the grubbettes. "They are so mean," she told Alan Franks. "They continually play the sisterhood card. 'I am a woman too,' they say, 'and we have these things in common.' And then they abuse it so cynically in print. Maybe their editor has said, 'Go out and find out the what, why and where.' I suspect not. I think it's them saying, 'I am really going to get to this woman and find out what she's like, and then knit it up into some shoddy little cardie and show it to the public,' and that's what they do. They are closer to home, and they know exactly the point at which to put the knife in. They wouldn't do it to your face. They reserve that for the page and for their own gender. It's not just me. They give the same treatment to others as well. I don't know what generates it. I don't care what their agenda is. I just know it's there and I see the same old names delivering the same old stuff. I try to be articulate and answer what I am asked about, but the grubbettes aren't content and always manage to produce a parting shot which is unkind."

The sour aftertaste left by the experience made Rigg more wary at revealing herself for public scrutiny. "It's as though there really is something remarkable about me to be chewed over, when there probably isn't," she said. "So I will remain as private as possible until the day I die, which means I shall never write an autobiography."

After suffering through the emotional abyss of betrayal and divorce, the next chapter in Diana's life would be a story of personal and professional redemption.

CHAPTER THIRTEEN

• • • •

PERHAPS the hardest thing for many women when ending a long-term relationship isn't the mere emotional blow of losing a lover and companion from your daily life but having to reassess who you are in the context of the world at large. It is a post-feminist reality that many women's sense of self, and self-worth, is inextricably tied to whether or not they have a man by their side. They have come to view themselves and their lives through the prism of their marriage and as such find it uncomfortable being—and being seen as—a single individual. Diana Rigg had no such issues; she always retained her individuality even while engaging in the compromises that are a necessary part of any union, which is why to many she was a feminist icon.

"I'm not exactly a feminist," she demurred in a 1990 *San Francisco Herald* interview. "I just find the female condition more interesting than the male. I just think we've got more to deal with. It's absolutely unquestioned that we can. But we have to prove that we can—without changing around us. And I'm a great believer in achieving without concessions." Diana also suggested that some of the misconceptions about her stemmed from her candor: "I'm just articulate, and people find that frightening. Actually, I'm very practical and down-to-earth. Most actresses are, because they have to be."

Rigg was equally down-to-earth, and unequivocal, in her mothering philosophy. "The most important thing you can teach your child is that there is only one of them on the face of the earth, and that they are extremely precious, not just to you, their parents, but to themselves, and must recognize how divinely individual they are," she stressed to writer David Nathan. "It's so incredibly shortsighted of any government not to see that the children are our greatest asset."

It is no small irony that one of Rigg's greatest concerns was how much influence pop culture might have on her daughter's perceptions of life and love. She explained: "Real romance starts in the head deep inside you, but if you are persuaded from a very early age to see it through a soft-focus lens, you get a false image. Possibly, parents are not quite as fierce as they might be about what children should watch, so they grow up with ludicrous ideas about love. That's why marriage is having trouble. That's why young people can't sustain a marriage, because they haven't had the time, the space, they haven't done the growing up to be able to determine for themselves what they care passionately about. Rachael is now reaching an age where, I think, she is affected by what she sees, and I shriek like a banshee that it's phony, false, pretence, rubbish."

Unwilling to leave it to chance, Rigg supervised what her teenager watched. "I say: 'You just can't watch it.' I don't equivocate," she explained. "If you do, you end up with a very confused child. It is not a specific film or television program I'm against. It's the easy-come, easy-go emotion they deal in." Diana was aware that other actors were complicit in the very pop-culture portrayals that so annoyed her but trusted her daughter to make the distinction. "She knows me as a person and she's seen me as an actress so she has seen the illusion, and hopefully she will be able to steer her way delicately through the rubbish," she said.

It wasn't as if Rigg was being sanctimonious; she simply felt it was her parental responsibility to instill a proper set of values, while at the same time nurturing an exceedingly close relationship with Rachael. "I can't pretend that I'm anything other than who I am, so I'm not about to," Rigg told Nigel Farndale. "Rachael is probably a better daughter to me than I was to my mother. I have always tried to be open with her. But I think I made mistakes. You do. But you just have to trust your instincts. I stopped my career because I couldn't bear not to be there. I don't think my profession made any difference with her, though. My divorce? I'm not sure."

With her marriage over and her daughter at boarding school, Rigg was ready to get back to work; specifically, she needed to be back onstage. "I began onstage, and I am much happier onstage than I am in front of a movie camera," she told *Harper's Bazaar*. "I've made a lot of rather bad movies, and I've been rather badly treated. I don't think I've entirely succeeded on film because the business of moviemaking is slightly victimizing. You do what you have to, but after three takes, one of which you think is best, the director will choose the other. Then comes the business of lighting and the final editing and all that. But when you're onstage from 7:30 P.M. until 10:30 P.M. curtain, it's in your hands and your hands entirely. I've never gotten over the fact that I feel not quite in command in film. It's simply to do with an appetite now for really good work in the final third of my life. The theater to me is home; in some curious way, I don't belong anywhere else."

Likewise, Diana wasn't sure that feature-film stars would ever truly feel comfortable on the classical stage. When asked if she thought someone like Brando could make it, she said, "I think an actor like Brando would make it anywhere. I don't know whether he would make it in the National Theatre. I don't know if he could come to terms with the fact of sharing a dressing room if he was number one.

"Most actors apologize for being actors, and, especially if they come from a working-class family, they apologize for getting large sums of money for what seems like two hours' work. I don't apologize for what I do at all. It's taken me years and years, and I work very hard at it. You spend a lot of time perfecting yourself and your looks and all that, and women are supposed to enjoy that rather more than men. But if you talk to makeup men, they will tell you that men are infinitely more vain than women in this business."

Rigg also found her male theater costars more amiable than her cinematic leading men. In thinking back over some of her more notable feature-film leading men—George Lazenby,

Oliver Reed and George C. Scott—she categorized them to the *Sunday Times* as, "in one way or another, all difficult leading men," but not as difficult as the men in the executive suites. "I never truly liked the movie business, and I still don't," she admitted. "It's the people. Not those on the studio floor; they are wonderful, and all masters of their art. But the people in the offices; they are a nightmare. I simply couldn't cope with Hollywood. I love watching the Oscars ceremony, I love film stars and I love what comes out of Hollywood. But heaven forfend I should ever be part of it."

Not that anyone was asking. Just when she needed most to get back to work for some emotional footing, there was nothing to be had. "It wasn't that I was going for parts and not getting them," she told the *Sun*. "I wasn't being offered anything at all." She was even turned down by the BBC when

Rigg as Cleopatra in *All for Love*

she applied to do a directing course there. She explained: "All actors go through quiet periods, but not many of them will talk about it. It's to do with the fact that when you're married, you become—well, I did—the married woman. If you do not pay your dues all the way along the line the theater is an unforgiving place, and rightly so. You have to be single-minded about it, and for a long time I was not. My daughter and domestic life came first. Then, when I shot my hand up and *adsum* [I'm here] and nobody wanted to know, I had to start from the bottom.

"Well, there was an old warhorse of a play, whose name I am not going to mention, and I thought, '*No.*' I swear it's nothing to do with being chic or smart or anything like that, just that, as I say, I want to be experimenting, rather than simply going through the motions."

She was given such an opportunity rather unexpectedly when contacted by Jonathan Kent, codirector of the Almeida, which in 1991 was a small, rather obscure 300-seat theater located in North London's Islington district (the equivalent of off, off, *off* Broadway). Kent was planning a production of *All for Love*, seventeenth-century playwright John Dryden's revamped version of Shakespeare's *Antony and Cleopatra*, and offered Rigg the starring role, for which she would earn about $300 a week. Diana jumped at the chance. "Because every woman of my age, if asked to do Cleopatra, would say, 'Yes, thank you very much,'" she explained.

The Almeida's space is so small rehearsals were conducted in another building down the road. With two dressing rooms, one for men and one for women, all the actors, headliners and bit players alike, were expected to share. "It's like being a walk-on at Stratford all over again," Rigg exclaimed—but in joy, not dismay. It was by-the-seat-of-your-pants theater, certainly done for love and not money, with everyone receiving the same £165 a week. It didn't matter to Diana, who was "suffused with gratitude" to Jonathan Kent.

Not only had he given her an opportunity to start "earning her dues" again, *All for Love* gave Rigg the chance to revisit one of her few stage disappointments. Six years earlier, she had appeared in a production of Shakespeare's *Antony and Cleopatra* that proved to be less than memorable. "I regret it," she admitted to David Nathan, "because it is a wonderful part and I would have loved to do it properly for the audience's sake, as much as mine. Still, a lot of Cleopatras have sunk without trace, barge and all." So she was also looking forward to having the opportunity to tackle the character again.

What she found particularly intriguing about Dryden's take on the legendary Egyptian queen was her earthiness. "Different cultures have seen Cleopatra so differently—she's been played old, young, scheming, ingenuous—that she has come to embody womanhood," Rigg observed later to Benedict Nightingale. "I like her. I like her a lot. She is witty, self-aware, ironic, deeply passionate—all the things I admire in women. And Dryden's Cleopatra is so much more fleshed than Shakespeare's. She's a quantum leap nearer to a woman. I feel I'm swimming in warm water. Shakespeare's women exist to represent eternal truths. But the most important thing in the character is the person, and I don't think Shakespeare really understood women. His Cleopatra is always conscious of her regality, especially at the end. In Dryden, she sits by Antony and says: 'Hail, dear relic of my immortal love.' There's an accessibility about it. You can feel the blood coursing through the veins. Somehow, for both Dryden and Shakespeare, it was the variability of women's emotions that was uppermost in their minds. We don't know what Shakespeare's knowledge of women was, but Dryden certainly had a passionate affair, so I suspect he knew rather more."

In listening to her describe Cleopatra, it's sometimes difficult to know where the character ended and Rigg herself began. "Cleopatra was a very truthful, down-to-earth, level-headed woman," Diana mused to the *Sunday Times*. "Dryden's Cleopatra finds it very hard to feign, as she calls it. Her love is worn on her sleeve. She is very passionate as, indeed, is Shakespeare's, but she is much more carnal. The sexuality between her and Antony is much more stated. Dryden took the humanist view of this couple; twentieth-century audiences will see less the spectacle and sweep of history than two people who made a terrible mistake for all the right reasons. But they did, in fact, conquer in the end because they became legendary." Rigg bristled at the suggestion that by accepting death, Cleopatra was ultimately a quitter: "Absolutely not; she recognized it as their destiny, hers and Antony's, to die together. That is not quitting. They had no alternative. They were besieged. They conquered Caesar by dying. It is not to say that one would do it oneself, but I can perfectly well understand."

"But you can't talk about it in terms of twentieth-century practicality," she stressed to Benedict Nightingale. "Dryden saw it as their destiny, that by dying together they'd conquer the world, which of course they did by becoming mythical figures. They overcame everything—time, civilization. Nowadays we're very pussyfooting about love, aren't we? I think of poor old Mr. Trump, writing out his marriage contract. It's a far cry from Antony and Cleopatra, who were of course worth forty-five Mr. Trumps. My Cleopatra never questions it: 'We have kissed away a kingdom, that's a trifle.' This is what we all want to hear, as the antithesis of what we read in the newspapers about Ivana's $28 million." The play's subtext of self-destructive but enduring love must have had a certain resonance with Diana at this point in her life. She said, "If you ask me whether I believe in the power of love, then Antony and Cleopatra's love is, I suppose, the archetypal story of two people who became immortal through it. I suppose the world needs that sort of story because it needs to believe that that sort of love exists. Romance has a hard time in this world. It is essential that people discover for themselves what is romantic. The trouble is that people aren't allowed to work it out for themselves because of the big and the little screens and music and all those insidious, persuasive tools of modern life."

In one scene of the play, Antony's wife, Octavia, confronts Cleopatra and says, "I would view nearer that face which has so long usurped my right." Cleopatra responds icily, "Had you known but half these charms, you had not lost his heart." Diana admitted to Pauline Peters it was one of her favorite moments in the play: "The wife and the mistress together. It's wonderfully funny. These two women are scrapping. There are all sorts of incidental ironies." It's no surprise, then, when

Rigg also acknowledges she identifies with Cleopatra "in every way."

Having a complex role to inhabit infused Rigg with an intensity and life force that was almost tangible, and she embraced the work process like a drowning man does a float. As she explained it, "Dryden is good to act in the sense that it's so glorious, but all the verse form is quite hard. It has to be in your bones. You can only put it there with sheer effort. I love this sort of hard work. It drags you up by the scruff of your neck." Although *All for Love* was giving her the chance to work some long-dormant dramatic muscles, Rigg was still able to put the importance of the role in perspective. "Always the particular one I'm doing is my favorite," she said. "I give it my total and utter loyalty at the time. I don't want to sound complacent, but I just love my work. I still feel a sense of relish whenever I go into the theater at night, and I love it when I look up at the curtain call and see all those spectral faces in the gods. I try not to see them as a body of people but as individuals, and I bless them every night."

Interestingly, Rigg believed that sometimes the best performances happened when the actors were physically and emotionally spent, such as during an evening performance after the opening matinee. "We will be slightly tired, and exciting things can happen onstage when actors are overstretched," she explained to the *Evening Standard*. "The things we have rehearsed will have become second nature, and there's a chance that we will make that quantum leap which is utter instinct."

It was somewhat fateful timing that Rigg suddenly found

herself associated with the Almeida, because it was then that the theater was in the middle of a budgetary crisis, having twenty percent of its public funding cut by a London city grants committee amid charges that it was elitist because of its classical fare. Diana found such thinking ludicrous. "There is no such thing as elitism because everything you see on the stage is understandable," Rigg told the *Sunday Times*. "All it requires is for someone to be prepared to try to understand it. It is that attempt to understand which travels the distance between what people are when they come into a theater and what they are when they leave, and contain rather more than they did when they came in."

The more pressing issue was the real possibility that the theater might have to shut its door for a year if the funding wasn't restored on appeal. "Most theaters fulfill their brief, and go out and get sponsorship," Rigg observed to John Walsh. "The Almeida has done its share through AT&T. But it seems confusing and unfair that a theater should be penalized for being successful on a shoestring. I cannot believe the condescension of some local councilor who talked about elitist theater. What is he suggesting? That the community of Islington cannot understand the plays that are on at the Almeida? That's an insult. But there, the theater has been whipped for years, and they're still whipping it." Rigg did more than simply talk about the problems of theater funding. She was still affiliated with Scotland's MacRoberts Centre and did her part in trying to secure support. "I spend my time going to boring dinners and chatting people up to get money for all sorts of projects," she explained. "I certainly wouldn't put the arts above schools or medical services in a scale of importance, but I do hold the view that they are nothing less than essential to the education and health of the country, in the broadest senses of those words."

Being back in the public eye meant having to deflect questions about the breakup of her marriage to Stirling the previous year. Although Rigg refused to be specific, her responses still offered a glimpse into her more private thoughts and emotions. "First of all it's a form of curiosity which I most dislike," Diana explained to Pauline Peters. "And I just feel passionately that one's private life is a lifeline. And were I to spill out to all and sundry, I would lose something of inestimable value. I think you are the sum of the way you have lived, what you've believed in. There's no such thing as transformation, and whatever the slings and arrows that happen in later life, it is garnering the philosophy you have amassed those years before that help you through it."

Rigg was more comfortable talking about the strength and comfort she had found in religion through recent trying times. "It's a rock against things that are so transitory," she said. "I admire people who can do it—survive the pain and betrayal there probably are in all marriages. But it must be worth it. I'm pretty old-fashioned about it; pretty Yorkshire. I've stayed on good terms with my former husband. I'm slightly aghast that you see before you a twice-divorced woman. Considering my background and my parents' stable, loving marriage, I'm rather appalled that mine didn't work. I'm shocked. It's not how I saw myself, how I imagined things would work out, not what I believe in."

For all her regret, Diana wasn't necessarily one to sit around and let the dust settle on her, either. When asked by Nigel Farmdale of the *Sunday Telegraph Magazine* if she still took lovers, Rigg again gracefully demurred: "I refuse to answer that question. It's very simple. If you are not married but you are lucky enough, as in my case, to have a child, a career and a life outside your career, then you can be happy. I see myself as being as happy—truly happy—as anyone can be, given those circumstances."

Like many who face the prospect of middle age without a spouse, Rigg drew support and companionship from her wealth of friends. Despite her fifty-three years, Diana could still leave men's tongues wagging, although she seemed, for the most part, disinterested in raging hormones. "I don't think that being desired is necessarily the most important thing," she remarked. "The most important thing is your own self-esteem. If that's based on somebody else desiring you, it is a load of old rubbish. Oh yeah. Somebody else's desire is going to disappear sooner or later—and what are you left with if that's all your reality is?" Besides, as she pointed out to the *Evening Standard*, to know her wasn't necessarily to like her. "No, I'm not being modest. I'm too proud. I can be arrogant as well, certainly short-tempered," she said.

Rigg's choler was evident in a run-in with a nonsmoker at a posh London restaurant. Several newspapers ran accounts of the incident, in which the Earl of Bradford was sitting down-wind from Dame Diana when she lit up a cigarette. When the Earl politely asked Rigg to put out her cigarette, she was not amused. As he explained, "I got an extremely dirty look.

She put it out, but with bad grace I thought. I remember it particularly because of the look I got from her. If I could have found a stone to crawl under I would have done. It was a look that said, 'You miserable little man, why are you spoiling my fun?'" The Earl felt he had a right to ask her to stop smoking because it was spoiling his meal. "She was next to my table," he said, "extremely close to me, and her cigarette smoke was going up my nose whilst I was trying to eat my main course."

When asked about the incident later, Diana seemed nonplussed. "I don't even remember the incident," she responded. "Most restaurants as a rule put smokers in one area and nonsmokers in another so the issue doesn't arise."

When pressed to reveal her perceived best qualities, Diana was thoughtful: "I'm very loving to the people I'm fond of. In all ways. I think loving is like a muscle. The more you exercise it, the more capacity you have for it—the more, the more, the more. I'm not talking about my domestic scene; I'm just talking about the business of loving colleagues, friends."

The importance of loving had long been a favorite topic of Diana's. Back in 1973 she had told writer Michael Kustow that one of her unfulfilled dreams was to develop a show about Sappho "and what she represented." Diana explained: "She settled on the island of Lesbos but the important thing about her isn't that she was a dyke. She celebrated love and loving; she loved men and she also loved women. This is a concept which we've absolutely lost in the twentieth century because everything has to be categorized by male and female, and anything in between is suspect, subject to one law or another, whether it's social disapproval or an actual law. And I'd like to examine that area between male and female, simply to do it as a celebration, a celebration of loving.

"The women writers we have . . . couldn't be more feminist and more masochistic. I want to get the female statement away from masochism. Extremism is exactly what I would like it *not* to be about—neither the extremes of male or female. I would like to walk into that land that nobody seems interested in, where loving matters, whether it be a man or a woman. It's much more positive than not loving."

Her next stage role would also explore the eternal themes of love, as well as loss and revenge, and would reestablish Rigg as one of the premiere theater actresses of her generation.

Chapter Fourteen

• • • •

A L L actors decry being stereotyped, claiming that by the very nature of being an actor, they can believably play any number of roles and character types. But there are certain roles that come along at certain times of an actor's life that simply resonate more within them because they are not only acting the part as written, they are reliving some of their personal history and infusing their interpretation with an inner emotional knowledge and familiarity that transcends mere acting into true performance art. For Diana Rigg, that role was Medea—whether she was willing to admit it or not.

In 1992, Jonathan Kent staged a production of Euripides' classic Greek tragedy, in which Medea wreaks the most horrible vengeance imaginable on her husband Jason for deserting her and marrying the king's daughter in a stroke of political ambition and expediency. She not only kills Jason's new wife but she murders her own children as well. It would have been disingenuous of the theater press to ignore the obvious similarities between the basic plot of *Medea*—wife loses husband to younger woman—and Rigg's own well-publicized marital problems. Even so, Rigg admitted being offended by suggestions that her characterization was so affecting because it had been drawn from life. "I get very miffed, yes," she said. "Medea was a rejected woman and I was a rejected woman, but that's as far as any connection went. Medea is a part any actress would want to play. I can't stand this idea that actors use the stage as therapy. How *dare* they! The art of the theater is too great to be abused like that."

However, she did allow that while playing Medea, she tapped into her darkest emotions in a way she hadn't been able to previously expose. "It was something to do with bottoming out; you have nothing to hide," she said. But had there been any excess emotional baggage, the role would have teetered dangerously close to psychodrama. "It's dreary to carry this stuff with you," she told Matt Wolf. "Obviously, I've felt a lot of Medea's emotions but not quite to the same degree. I have nothing to work out; I have no rage. Performance is a matter of developing and enlarging, but it begins and ends with the text. It's so psychologically pure that when Medea reaches that point, there are no alternatives; none."

Rigg maintained that, beyond a grasp of the emotional subtext, Medea required an accumulation of acting skills. "I suppose Medea should be played by a younger woman, but it is traditionally played by older women, and for good reason," she observed. "It requires a vast amount, technically and emotionally, and that only comes with years of practice." The role also required a significant amount of physical stamina and a daily preparation worthy of a world-class athlete. "The physical demands of playing the role are not unlike climbing a mountain every night," she explained. "It's like being a marathon runner. You have to husband your strength and be very careful not to tire yourself during the day; you must eat at the right time, because it is hopeless going onstage with a full stomach. The fact of the matter is, because I'm onstage all the time it's my energy that drives it. And if my energy is down, there ain't no drive. There's no point where you can sit back and say, 'That's it, I've done it;' it's such a mammoth part."

From the beginning, Diana knew that this role was a special opportunity, and there were times when she felt transformed. She told the *Boston Globe*, "There were times doing Medea that were sort of indescribable. Something takes over, you know not what. And, dear God, you wish it would happen every night, but it doesn't. But when it does, it's a miracle."

Rigg's portrayal of Medea was so searingly intense that audiences and critics were either riveted or turned off by its unrelenting rage. But by far, the vast majority of those who saw the performance rank it as legendary. British reviewer Neil Smith wrote: "Kent's production has taken a year to reach the West End, but it's well worth the wait. . . . And Diana Rigg, returning to the limelight after too many years away, turns in the kind of searing performance that leaves an indelible impression on the memory. With her face pinched with bile and her Amazonian frame garbed in the most unfetching robe imaginable (Paul Brown's drab designs may be authentic but they're not exactly catwalk material), Rigg captures all

© ROBBIE JACK / CORBIS

Diana Rigg as Medea with her ill-fated sons

the pain and pathos of Euripides' female fury. 'I know what I intend to do is wrong, but the rage in my heart is stronger than my reason,' she explains to the complicit chorus as she plots against her rival and prepares to slaughter her own children. . . . But for the raw power of Ms. Rigg's performance this is compulsive theatre: in the role of a lifetime she just keeps on getting better and better."

Helen Reid of the *Western Daily Press* agreed: "The staging is in a savage iron tank which clangs horribly as the characters rage and bang against it and the chorus is a band of three old crows who sing and chant and dance their dreadful warnings and at the center of all this is the chillingly powerful performance of Diana Rigg as Medea. Her role is unremittingly violent and passionate at full tilt for over an hour, yet her performance is never too melodramatic or exaggerated to destroy our belief in her: Euripides and the audience are meant to be on her side even though grief and rage have turned her into a monster. It is a remarkable piece of acting."

To some reviewers it seemed incongruous that Rigg managed to evoke sympathy for Medea, considering her actions. Charles Spencer of the *Daily Telegraph* observed: "Her Medea was marvelous—remarkable for the mixture of restraint and passion. It is easy to play Medea as a noisily emoting monster. Rigg achieved the far harder task of making the viewer both respect and pity a child killer. Her anguish as she showered her sons with kisses and talked of 'the gentle smell of childhood' created a wrench of sympathy that seemed inconceivable when you considered the monstrosity of the crime she was about to commit."

Finding herself once again in the public eye, Diana seemed more at ease and was even willing to answer questions, albeit indirectly, that tiptoed past the professional into her private life. Now, having more distance from the breakup of her marriage to Archie, Rigg admitted just how despondent she had been in the immediate aftermath and how she had even sought counsel from a therapist. She described the therapy experience to Grace Bradberry: "Absolutely pointless. The first person I went to see made me lie down. I remember looking at these blinds, and the silence grew. It was eighty pounds an hour, and it had to be Wednesdays between two and three. That was my time, and if I didn't come I'd still have to pay her."

Perhaps the most lingering discomfort she felt was that she carried the label of "twice-divorced woman." As she explained, "It's got to do with how you see yourself. I saw myself marrying late and maintaining a marriage because I think those that do are laudable. The older you get, the more you realize that marriage—two disparate people coming together and living together for forty, maybe fifty years—is something of a miracle." It was also something she had resigned herself to not achieving, announcing that there were no more marriages in her future: "Not in a million years, no. I don't think I could possibly, I couldn't bear it." Beyond not wanting to endure the agony of another divorce, Rigg was of an age where independence loomed large. "I do exactly what I want, when I want, and I don't answer to anybody, which is largely what marriage is about," she said. "Not to say that I didn't grieve at the end of the marriage; I certainly did, but having come out of that phase I then discovered the huge pluses of being a single woman with enough money to do what you want. It's great! I've stopped rebelling now because, obviously, I can lead my life as I please. I was incredibly lucky that when the marriage ended I refound my career and all the things I'd enjoyed all those years earlier—like freedom."

Not to mention critical acclaim for her acting. Her performance in *Medea* earned Rigg the Evening Standard Award, Britain's version of a Tony, and a nomination for a Laurence Olivier Award and prompted an offer to bring the production to Broadway. It would be Diana's first time back on the New York stage in almost two decades. The reception to the play was equally enthusiastic, and reviewers seemed in awe.

"Mountain climbers have Everest. Swimmers have the English Channel. Actresses have Medea," said the *New York*

Times' David Richards. "The title character of Euripides' tragedy is one of the huge, ravenous roles of dramatic literature. It
will take everything a performer can give, then ask for more.
Sheer talent is not enough. Courage and a certain reckless-
ness are required to conquer it. A wild and exotic creature
who knows potions that cure and poisons that kill, Medea is
also a forsaken wife and tortured mother. She is one of us and
not like us at all.

"In the London-born production that began a limited
Broadway engagement last night at the Longacre Theater,
Diana Rigg brings a blazing intelligence and an elegant feroc-
ity to the part. . . . For the actress, who has always managed
to suggest impeccable breeding even when she is behaving
abominably, the evening is a triumph. . . . Unlike Zoe Caldwell,
who emphasized the sexuality of the character, Ms. Rigg sees
Medea as a woman of restless intellect. A passionate sense of
injustice propels Ms. Rigg. . . . Ms. Rigg, who has always had
a wry wit, does not forgo it here. In addition to the knife in
the folds of her robe, irony is one of her weapons. Medea, a
victim, is also a victimizer. The contradictions are tantalizing.
I'd want to see her if I were you."

Rigg found herself the center of media attention and
made herself accessible. For as tense as Diana sometimes felt
with British press, particularly women, she seemed especially at ease with "foreign" journalists. "There are no rules of
decency with English women journalists, and no manners—
unlike Americans," she explained. Rigg took no offense that
many regarded *Medea* as her comeback. "It's hard for women
to get the balance between their lives and careers right," she

observed. "I don't have scads of children. I only have one, and you can't afford to play around with that. . . . Often there is a casualty; it's either the career or the child. I preferred that the casualty was my career.

"Many years ago, when I was extremely young, I was playing in a company, and the leading lady, whom I admired and still do, invited me back to her flat one night. It was full of artifacts and bits and pieces of her travels and tours and shows. And that was all! I remember thinking, '*I don't want to wake up like this. I don't. I'm not interested.*'" Which is why she takes no offense to criticism that she might actually be an underachiever. "They're absolutely right," she says. "I could have gone on and done greater and greater things. But I didn't. It's as simple as that."

She even answered the inevitable *Avengers* questions with good humor and thoughtfulness, noting that many of the people coming to see her on Broadway were doing so primarily to see Emma Peel. "There is an instance of people getting to see a Greek classic which they would not otherwise have seen. I say terrific. It's all a matter of how fame translates into another sphere, and this is a very good instance," she explained. It also pleased Diana that her TV fans would get to see her in a theater context. "There are times when one thinks: '*I've been around for forty years and some people think* The Avengers *is the sum of what one's done,*'" she admitted to Peter Calder. "And the fact of the matter is it happened thirty years ago. But I can't complain because it certainly put me on the map. There are things one has done in the past that one would rather weren't resurrected. But *The Avengers* has kept its style."

And in the larger scheme of her career, Rigg has kept Peel in appropriate perspective. "To a certain extent, Peel has followed me. I think one can never lose a role to which one has been attached professionally if that role introduced you to a large public. And the part did me far more good than harm," she told Allan Brown. "I acknowledge what it did for me, I acknowledge the place it has in Britain's heart or whatever; I'm happy with it. But when people ask me to sign their *Avengers* pictures I can't because it makes me feel such a phony. Those pictures aren't me; they're me thirty years ago and sometimes that can be painful, or irrelevant. Let's face it. I looked better forty years ago than I do now, but I don't find it a matter of anguish. Actually, when I see pictures of myself then I always regard her as another person."

But the continuing interest amazed her. "Do you know I still get very passionate letters from small Japanese gentlemen? In America it's a sort of cult. They bring it on at 11:30 at night, along with horror movies and Carole Lombard. It's rather horrendous to be a cult in your own lifetime and to actually see yourself in black-and-white. I look like early Joan Crawford, lipstick up to there," she jokes.

Whatever reservations she had about her sixties fashion sense being perpetuated on U.S. cable channels, Rigg was more than happy to greet well-wishers who gathered outside the stage door, and she scored big points with New Yorkers for her gracious interest. She would stick her head out a window overlooking the exit and tell the people waiting she'd be down shortly. Then she would patiently sign every autograph request and spend a few moments talking to each person. To the surprise of everyone, while other actors were loaded into chauffeur-driven town cars, Diana would then take off walking down the street and disappear into the crowded night.

But Rigg firmly believed in living her life and refused to let her recognizability hinder her or prevent her from pursuing any interest. Rigg once told writer Andy Holden that when she arrived to work in a new city, she made a point of exploring it: "I grab whatever time I have. I'm a great walker so I'll walk over the city. When I check in I get a map and then explore. I always go to the museum. I always try and find an antique shop and buy if I see something. I love the galleries and I'll try and see what the young artists are doing."

While in New York for *Medea*, when she wasn't engaged in promoting the play and had time to herself, Rigg could often be found spending the afternoon in the New York Public Library reading books of poetry and researching a new book she was working on, an anthology of poems about the British countryside. "I discovered that, largely, I prefer research to everything else," she noted. "It's like you're a pig on a truffle hunt, and it's so exciting—reading, reading, reading and finding what you want."

The premise of the book is looking at the British countryside as seen through the poet's eye, "from early medieval texts to the modern day," she explained. "What fascinated me was reading a stanza of poetry and having this moment of recognition: '*Yes, I've seen that. Yes, I know what they're talking about.*' I take a metaphoric day in each season—and I've found poems about not just the seasons, the flowers, the trees, but the sporting pursuits, the animals and the insects. For example, there's a wonderful nineteenth-century poem by somebody called Lord de Tabley on a spider. I had great fun pulling all these threads together, if you like." The book, *So To The Land: Anthology of Co*, was released in late 1994 to positive critical notice.

Just as she had won critical raves in London, when it came time for the Tony nominations, Diana found herself nominated for Best Actress in a Drama. With *Passion, Beauty and the Beast, Angels in America: Perestroika* and *Medea* among the more notable hits, 1994 was a vibrant year on Broadway. It wasn't the first time Rigg had been nominated, but the buzz on Broadway had her as the runaway favorite to take home the award. And then, a day before the Tonys were to be awarded, came news from England that managed to put Diana's excitement about the Tonys on stunned hold: it had been leaked to the British press that Queen Elizabeth was going to name Diana Rigg a Dame Commander of the British Empire. When the cast heard the news, they converged on Rigg's dressing room and treated her to a reworked version of Rodgers and Hammerstein's "There is Nothing Like a Dame" in honor of the occasion. Diana's reaction was to burst into tears of joy and gratitude. The next evening, Rigg was awarded the Tony, completing one of the most memorable professional weekends of her career.

Backstage after the awards, Rigg was effusive but clearly ready to go home, having announced that she would be closing *Medea* in two weeks to return to England. "Because I'm a very tired dame, and the voice is tired, and I want to go home and have a bit of a rest," she said. When asked by an apparently clueless American journalist if she had thanked the Queen for naming her a Dame, Rigg graciously joked, "No, I didn't phone her—she doesn't take calls." Later, at the after party, Rigg was her festive self, laughingly wondering aloud about the finer points of being a Dame. "I think it means I won't be able to say fuck anymore," she mused. Rigg was one-upped by another actress who quipped, "Actually, I think it means you can say any fucking thing you want."

Rigg returned home and, after a brief rest, found herself with not a lot to do work-wise. Amazingly, despite her success with *Medea*, Rigg returned to England without any immediate prospects. "When I again put my hand up, still nothing," she said. The ceremony making her a Dame took place November 8, and afterwards, Dame Diana recounted a brief conversation with the monarch: "The Queen asked me what I was working on at the moment and I told her I was an unemployed Dame."

But Rigg didn't stay unemployed for long. Thanks to *Mother Love* and *Medea*, it seemed Rigg had established herself as the *de rigeur* new villainess among TV producers. "They're all old bags but it's just what I keep getting offered," she observed. "The offers have kept rolling in, and I believe in working. I've just been jolly lucky; at a time when you're considered over-the-hill, I was able to notch these up. They do say the profession gets increasingly difficult, but my career seems to have been inside out; I'm playing the bigger parts now that I'm older. That's probably right because I wasn't ready for them before, so I'm grateful for them now."

"Anyway, I'd always rather play a baddie than a goodie.

They're just juicier, better roles and stronger women for the most part," she noted to Peter Calder. Nor was she concerned that on TV, fewer leading-lady roles came her way anymore. "I want to spend more time playing character parts," she commented. "I want to be the Denholm Elliott of the film world."

After playing supporting roles in various miniseries and TV movies, including *Moll Flanders*, Danielle Steele's *Zoya* and *Samson and Delilah*, Rigg sunk her acting chops into a role she sought out as soon as she learned a new film adaptation of Daphne du Maurier's gothic thriller, *Rebecca*, was being filmed.

In the U.S. in 1940, the book had been made into a feature film by Alfred Hitchcock that starred Joan Fontaine, Laurence Olivier and Judith Anderson and won the Academy Award for Best Picture. In the movie, Fontaine starred as a reserved young woman from a modest background who meets and falls in love with the wealthy and dashing widower Maxim de Winter. Although he still grieves over his wife Rebecca who died a year earlier, Maxim impulsively proposes and they marry. But once the new Mrs. de Winter arrives at Maxim's estate, called Manderley, she senses something sinister going on. Her primary adversary is the mysterious housekeeper, Mrs. Danvers, played by Dame Judith Anderson, who had been with Rebecca since she was a teenager and who resents anyone trying to take her place. Eventually, the shocking truth about Rebecca is revealed—she was a horrible person who drove Maxim to murder her. The new Mrs. de Winter accepts her husband despite his crime. Mrs. Danvers, however, goes over the edge and sets Manderley on fire, only to get trapped and die in the flames.

The role of Mrs. Danvers was too tasty for Rigg to pass up. "I think it's fascinating," she said. "Here is a woman who has served somebody else for most of her life to the point that she doesn't have a life of her own. I love the complexities of that sort of character. Mrs. Danvers worshipped Rebecca with absolute and total devotion." Rigg felt the television version had more complexity than Hitchcock's version: "Since it's based on the book, it adds more depth than you find in the Hitchcock movie, which is based on the play. There was a book first, then there was a play, and Hitchcock could only get the rights to the play. The public wants the characters to be fully explored and explained psychologically."

To portray the character, Rigg fleshed together a back story for Mrs. Danvers. She explained: "In those days, all the housekeepers were called Mrs. whether they were married or not. It was the custom. I suspect that Mrs. Danvers was not married and had never been married. She had looked after Rebecca since Rebecca was twelve. I suspect that Mrs. Danvers' love for Rebecca probably bordered on the lesbian, but Mrs. Danvers was not aware of it herself. I hope that's what comes across." Just as Medea's crime was inevitable, Rigg says Mrs. Danvers' torching the house also makes perfect psychological sense. "With the revelation of Rebecca and how Rebecca died, Rebecca's ghost is gone from Manderley, and Mrs. Danvers can't bear that Manderley now carries on without her," she explained.

Rigg told producers part of her interest in pursuing the

© ROBBIE JACK / CORBIS

Diana Rigg appears in a National Theatre production of *Mother Courage and Her Children*

role was that she liked "the opportunity of reexamining icons." As she put it, "Every generation has the right to do that. I love these roles, because it brings back a style of acting that went out for years and years. The trend was to glance at an emotion and glance off it, with suggestions but never any overt demonstration. I think you've got to be able to do both, because that's the nature of people."

Even though Rigg repeatedly wished wistfully for a comedy, her next two stage roles were angstfests. At the National, she tackled Bertolt Brecht's antiwar drama, *Mother Courage and Her Children*, the story of Anna Fierling, called Mother Courage, who follows the armies back and forth across Europe during the Thirty Years' War, selling provisions from her canteen wagon. Over the years, Anna loses all her children in the war but survives by doggedly hanging on to her wagon, which is her sole means of support. "She's like a steamroller through the play," observed Rigg. "She's just inexorable. Even at the end, when her daughter has died, she gets up and starts pushing that cart again." Although this hardly sounds like a laugh riot, Rigg maintained it's not all sturm and drang. "She has this rough humor, a stubborn refusal to accept defeat, and a habit of talking about people as if they're not there—all very northern," Diana noted to Jonathan Croall, referring to her Yorkshire upbringing. "Because it's about a woman pulling a cart round the stage for three and a half hours, everybody assumes that it's a megaglum play, right? Yet Brecht himself kept on saying that you should have fun in rehearsals—though with some of the adaptations you read, I don't see how you could. People stood in such awe of him, they didn't associate him with humor, which was wrong. The same happens with Chekhov: his plays have this aura around them of classic in another language. As a result they can seem fusty and dusty, so that it's like watching marionettes rather than real people.

"The one thing that Brecht didn't want is for you to be remotely sentimental at any point. Anyway, I hate it when actors play for sympathy."

Breaking with tradition, Diana refused to portray Anna "like an old drudge." She said in a *Stagewrite* interview, "Now I certainly won't be the most glamorous of women onstage, but I see no reason to look like a bag lady—on the contrary, I shall be quite gaily dressed. She's been around, has Mother Courage: she's got three children by three different husbands, and sex is not something unknown to her. Nor for that matter is she past it now, otherwise the cook and the chaplain wouldn't like being around her so much."

This was her first stage production since becoming a Dame and Rigg had obviously given some thought to the reasons behind the honor: "They just say, would you like to be a Dame? Then you have this conversation with yourself: *'Why me, and what difference will it make?'* I suspect it was a mixture of two things. One, that I played largely classic roles in subsidized theater, which meant that I was, if you like, not taking from the theater but giving to it. I suspect that it was partly the fact that I've been around a long time. But also, I work quite hard on the business of finding sponsorship for the arts and also that I sit on various boards and campaign and raise money for the arts. You get a medal, which the Queen pins on. You put it on at really official functions, when it says at the bottom of the invitation, 'Medals will be worn.' What difference has it made? Absolutely none." That was largely true because Rigg did not want her title to interfere with her theater experience. She explained, "It's a great honor, obviously, but I don't use the title in the theater. I prefer to be called Miss Rigg because I think, above everything else, the democracy of the stage should be upheld. We're all on the stage together. We all need each other, and I like that parity."

Her next Almeida production, *Who's Afraid of Virginia Woolf?*, made *Mother Courage* seem like a Noel Coward romp. Edward Albee's verbal slugfest is between history professor George—played by David Suchet, television's Hercule Poirot—and his wife Martha, the daughter of the university president, who emotionally dismember each other throughout the wee hours of the morning after a faculty party. The play was so physically and emotionally demanding that Rigg had to spend her day off recuperating. "Martha just eats into your life," she explained. "All of us in the play find our lives circumscribed by this performance, every evening, six nights a week and twice on Saturday, which means that Sunday is a complete wipeout. I would drag myself out of bed on Sunday and drive into the depths of the Dorset countryside. It was like losing yourself. I shed what I'd had to carry for months in the glory of those timeless trees and flowers. The country replenishes me."

While promoting the play, Rigg talked about the lure of theaters such as the Almeida: "Again and again actors, directors and designers return to work at the Almeida. The pay is Equity minimum and the conditions backstage are basic. So why are we there? Quite simply because the work comes first." Rigg frequently pointed out that garbage collectors made fifty percent more per week than actors at the Almeida. "It's all they can afford to pay. You have to subsidize work like this by doing TV work and commercials when you can get it," she said in an interview with the Press Association news agency. "When I was doing *Medea* in New York it transpired that one actress could only afford to be in the show because she had just done a series of well-paid ads, another because she had recently picked up a lot of money through a singing engagement, and so on."

It bothered Rigg that some actors equated their low wages with the worth of their profession and the stereotype of actors being somewhat unstable. "That they're damaged people, desperate for attention . . . absolute rubbish," she fumed to Allan Brown. "If you have a natural fascination for the human condition in its myriad forms, then you'll be an actor. Exhibitionist? I suppose you could call it that. But

Rigg in the Almeida Theatre production of
Who's Afraid of Virginia Woolf?

performing, standing up and being seen, has been an impetus for thousands of years, since before Christ." Her passion for her profession is why she vowed to "fight like stink in every corner" to have their lot improved "with candor and not much reticence."

To that end, Rigg was chairwoman of a Scottish arts center which had budgeted money to create a children's theater. "I'm passionate about that," she said, "the educative qualities of theater that spark the imagination in children. It gives them an arena for self-expression that maybe they don't have at home."

In 2001, Rigg would cause a stir and ruffle some feathers when she complained publicly about conditions at the National Theatre. "We're like battery hens at the National," she said in an interview for the National's members-only newsletter, referring to the Spartan dressing rooms. "They're completely without character, very noisy and with little space or decent light. As actors we don't expect to be pampered. But we have to be on top form to go out there and do it. The conditions are absolutely ludicrous for a theater built from scratch. It makes me cross every time I enter the building."

A spokesman for the National Theatre admitted the backstage conditions were "not terribly plush." He added, "They are very, very Spartan. We are an ensemble company. Rooms backstage are more functional, not like some in the West End where stars have large rooms, sofas, gilt mirrors and lots of folderol. Ours are adequate, and actors put up with them."

Working on two strenuous plays back-to-back had taken its toll, and when the run of *Who's Afraid of Virginia Woolf?*

ended, Rigg took a vacation and a break from the stage. "The stage is my first love, but I've done Mother Courage and Martha both within a year, and I just think I need a change," she said. But being on a self-imposed hiatus didn't mean that Diana was idle. After flying to New York to promote the U.S. broadcast of *Rebecca*, a performance that would win Rigg that year's Best Supporting Actress in a Miniseries Emmy, she treated herself to a Caribbean vacation, then flew to Washington where she presented Sir Derek Jacobi with the Sir John Gielgud Award at the Folger Library's sixty-fifth anniversary celebration.

New York columnist "Suzy" (Aileen Mehle) reported: "In a stunning Saint Laurent with an infinitesimal skirt, Diana made a speech almost as short as her skirt. She managed to be both witty and scholastic at the same time, the dear girl. The rapt audience managed to listen to her and stare at her famous legs at the same time. (They, the legs, haven't changed a whit since she played the super-sexy Emma Peel sewn into a black bodysuit in that famous TV series, "The Avengers.") Never one to rest on her laurels—or for that matter her bed—too long, Diana was up in the morning for an 8 a.m. breakfast at the White House with Hillary Clinton and such guests as . . . the British ambassador and his wife, Buffy and Bill Cafritz and others too privileged to mention."

Feeling refreshed, Rigg was ready to return to the stage. As she approached her sixtieth birthday, it was obvious she was starting to increasingly think of her place in the continuum and of what responsibility she had to the generations behind her. "That's what it's about, it's a long-distance race," she observed. "You've got to put the baton, clear and straight, into the hand of the young person who's at your shoulder, and turn to them and say, 'Go!'" But she worried that some of the learning opportunities she enjoyed were diminishing. "I'm a company person, bred in the company ethos," she said. "We rather mourn the demise of companies in the truest sense. The National Theatre calls itself a company but it isn't. Each play is cast afresh; they don't always use whoever's in-house, as it were, which I think is a great mistake. In that respect the young aren't nurtured. A lot of actors go straight into telly from drama school and don't get much experience of stage. I think the stage is much more collaborative in spirit than telly and film." She told Andrew Holden the greatest value of repertory was that "it has you working at your optimum and that's what this business is about." She added, "It's not about standing on your back foot and delivering a performance that is tried, true and tested and you've done a thousand times before, but pushing yourself further each time."

That desire to keep stretching herself creatively led Diana to toy with the idea of directing. "But then," she said, "I realized what a dreadfully onerous responsibility it is. You've got actors' careers on the line. It's a very courageous business, ours, and I thought, *I can't handle that.*'" In the end, it always came back to the stage. Rigg explained, "If you want to prolong your professional life, the theater is going to do it for you, not film. Generally speaking, if you get to seventy in films you're out of it, apart from the odd walk-on or miraculous part, whereas if you've got as far as seventy on the stage you're honored and you are the sum of your parts."

Her instinctual, almost primal, draw to the theater and belief in its promise of longevity is one reason why she hadn't felt compelled to go back to Hollywood and avenge her *Diana* failure. "It sounds a strange thing to say but I think you've got to be competitive in order to enjoy America and, although I'm in a competitive profession, I'm not deeply competitive. I'm jolly lucky to have got as far as I have with as little competition as I have inside me," she observed.

But for all she had achieved, Dame Diana seemed genetically incapable to rest on her successes. Driven to keep growing as an individual and as a professional, she continued to seek out new challenges even as she quietly began to prepare for a life out of the public eye.

CHAPTER FIFTEEN

• • • •

D A M E Diana had always maintained she wanted her daughter to forge her own path and never overtly nudged Rachael toward the stage. But she didn't need to. Not only had Rachael inherited her mother's stature, her high cheekbones and her coloring, she also inherited her passion for acting. In September 1996, Rachael made her stage debut as Desdemona in the National Youth Theatre's production of *Othello*. Although nobody could ever accuse Rigg of being a stage mother, Rachael recalls, "My mother gave me the script of *Othello* for my birthday, with lots of Post-it notes offering suggestions about posture and things." Displaying a very Riggesque flash of independence, Rachael added, "I do take her advice—when I agree."

Although her daughter might not have been the most eager of students to hear Rigg's accumulated theatrical wisdom, in 1998 Dame Diana suddenly found herself sought after by academia and relished taking on the new challenge of teaching young acting hopefuls.

In October, she was appointed Chancellor of the University of Stirling, the first woman to hold the position in the university's then thirty-one-year history. For the previous ten years Rigg had been chairman of the school's MacRobert Arts Centre. At the installation ceremony, attended by more than 300 guests, Rigg said, "The academic world is a far cry from that of a thespian, although both have a lot of learning to do. I hope to be a credible chancellor to Stirling University and to enjoy and learn about this new world. I hope to uphold this very great faith that has been placed in me." Typically, Rigg intended to be as involved as she could and not be chancellor in name only. "It's a great honor!" she remarked. "Mainly, I'll be there during degree ceremonies and I'll represent the principal at events to which he can't get. Having said that, the university understands that, because I'm a working actress, I can't give the time I'd like to."

But among her top priorities was to encourage local citizens to show more support. "It's a very interesting situation in Stirling, with the MacRobert," she observed. "People in Scotland are slightly diffident about going to see drama at a venue that's run by a university; there's a perception that what's put on will be too highbrow. It's a problem, but an interesting problem, so I'll be looking into how we can change that."

The position, mostly a ceremonial post, was intended to raise the profile of the university and give it a well-known figurehead to be trot out during official events. Having someone of Rigg's stature was a coup for the small college. The university's Senior Deputy Principal, Professor Mike Jackson, enthused, "The nomination of Diana Rigg as chancellor has caught the imagination. It has not simply been welcomed by staff of all ages and all backgrounds, but rather welcomed with acclaim."

Although her focus would be on theater, Rigg also made it a point to familiarize herself with all the curriculums offered. "I'm steadily working my way through all the departments in the university so that I know what I'm chancellor of," she said. "The fact of the matter is I'm fascinated by just about anything. Aquaculture! Ask me something about aquaculture."

At the time, Rigg still called Stirling her home. Despite the end of her marriage, she still held the land dear. Every year, Rigg drove to the grave of Stirling's Aunt Irene, whom she "loved very much," on the anniversary of her death, and was continually affected by the Scottish landscape. "It's the most wonderful drive in the world," she said. "Up through Glen Coe. Absolutely terrifying! I play tapes of bagpipe music as I go through the glen; that gives me goose pimples. Then up through Inverness. Everything becomes softer, the air, the light. Then you go up a hill and get your first glimpse of the sea. Utterly ravishing! We had wonderful times in Morar and Mallaig. Irene would barter for everything. She'd swap someone lettuces for crayfish.

"And I was so proud to have been chieftain at the Bridge of Allan and Callander Games. I love those agricultural shows full of men in Barbour jackets. And the goat women—these lovely women lead their goats round the

Highland shows on pieces of string. They're my favorite." Then in November 1998, England's Oxford University hired Rigg as its new professor of theater studies. Technically a "visiting professor," her duties included holding master classes and getting other notable directors, actors and producers to show up as guest speakers. In the *Sunday Times*, Oxford's Dr. Paul Flather defended the growing tendency to hire celebrities to fill temporary posts because it would mean "packed lecture halls and new ideas." He explained, "Oxford is home to the most vibrant and challenging debates. It is only natural for us to want to attract the most exciting, lively and prestigious figures from all over the world to confront us and to inspire us."

But it turned out that Oxford students could be as fickle as audiences. Although her first lecture played to a packed house, the attendance of subsequent presentations dwindled to where at one, only eleven students showed up, prompting Diana to advertise in the Drama Society newsletter.

Perhaps it was simply a matter of regular access breeding indifference, because when Dame Diana showed up at Harvard for a special lecture on diction, people were literally hanging off the walls, fire marshall be damned. Rigg, who was in Boston to tape intros for *Mystery!*, stressed the importance of proper theatrical vocal techniques to members of the faculty and their invited guests. "Voice has the capacity to hold an audience, to illuminate a text or to spark imagination," she asserted.

According to Miranda Daniloff, Rigg demonstrated several vocal exercises, such as using pauses to "snap your audience to attention." Inflection was everything, Rigg said: "It can convey commitment, passion and an interest in the subject, while monotones are a sure way to fail. It isn't an optimistic way to address people. Sooner or later it's rather depressing." Dame Diana revealed that Former British Prime Minister Margaret Thatcher had taken voice lessons to lower the register of her voice to sound more authoritarian. She wryly noted that, in general, politicians pay particular attention to vocal techniques because it makes "their insincerity come across as sincerity."

She finished by observing that anyone who works in front of an audience, be he actor or teacher, can improve the quality of his work by mastering his vocal talents. "For those of you who speak regularly, your voice and your body are there to serve your text," she said.

And unlike many drama teachers, Rigg was in the enviable position of being able to demonstrate her lessons on the stage and in front of the camera. In 1998, she signed on to star in the British series *The Mrs. Bradley Mysteries* as Jazz Age crime-solving psychologist Adela Bradley. The television show was based on author Gladys Mitchell's book series.

"She is great fun to play," said Rigg. "She was a liberated woman, which was rare in her time. She's endlessly witty and has pots of money. You'll see vintage cars and fine old English houses. That was nice. Also nice are the clothes I wear, the 1920s costumes. It's the absolutely most perfect work for me at this age." This was in part because she got to play someone her own age. "I'm not interested in playing younger than myself," she explained, "although you do in the classics, necessarily. It's too much of a schlep, with all that makeup. In *The Mrs. Bradley Mysteries* I gave the makeup twenty minutes, maximum. I was always like that—I couldn't be bothered."

Despite being of the same age and possessing the same wit, Rigg insists, "In terms of acting, I have to travel some to play her—Adela Bradley is not me. But I like the fact that she is unexpected. She is not formulaic. I like the asides she makes to the camera. It is a wonderful opportunity to express her thoughts, particularly in the twenties and thirties when social manners were pretty strict. You can break that by turning to the camera and saying, 'I am having dinner with very boring people.' You can be outrageous without being a monster."

Sometimes, Mrs. Bradley's dialogue seems to have been handcrafted for Dame Diana, such as when Adela observes: "I'm never entirely sure if I'm famous or notorious. Someone once said 'fame' is to live in poverty and end up as a statue. Naturally, I prefer to be notorious."

Actually, the argument could be made that Dame Diana had happily achieved both fame and notoriety. Certainly she had achieved respect as one of England's greatest stage actors. But even so, Rigg always felt she could do better, which is why she agreed to reprise her role as Phedre (Phaedra), the apparently widowed queen who falls in love with her stepson and then finds out that her husband is still alive. Dame Diana had originally played the part twenty-three years earlier at the National Theatre but admitted she had always been a bit disappointed in her portrayal. "Now that I'm older I think I have a better understanding of the tragedy," she told the *Weekly*

Telegraph. "Then, I had a fear of revealing myself, my emotions. I felt somehow that I ought to be a bit ashamed of them—rage, jealousy, guilt. You can only play the role if you give full vent to them. Also, I have a stepson, so yes I can relate to that, too—but not—if you see what I mean."

After sending her husband off to his death and suffering the guilt-ridden emotional conse-quences of her actions,

Rigg as Phedre

Phedre welcomes her own death. Not only was Rigg better able to express her emotions in the role, she had a greater compassion for Phedre's mindset when approaching death. She explained: "On the one hand Phedre knows her death is predestined by the gods. On the other she is fighting it. She thinks she can prevent it. I believe you have to take hold of death. But, then, I've never had to face it so how dare I say that? Come the time, how can you possibly know how strong your belief will be?"

While some actors of Rigg's stature played up the part of grande dame off stage, Rigg dismissed such a scenario and denied she commanded awe from her younger costars. "No, they are all too busy wrestling with their own demons," she said. "Besides, I still suffer from appalling nerves. I always arrive too early, and before I go on I just sit in my dressing room and listen to the crowds arriving. *Murmur, murmur.* I have to tell myself, *'How daaare you be nervous? Just get on with it and stop making a fuss.'* I suspect it is the Yorkshire voice again."

While Rigg might try to proclaim that she held no particular sway over the youth of Gen-X, *Playboy* magazine sent a forceful reminder that to baby boomers she was still an icon, by voting her number seventy-five on their list of the "100 Sexiest Stars of the Century." Although she found it bemusing, she admitted to Benedict Nightingale she was flattered: "Wouldn't you be? I'm not in a position to judge, but for somebody who has never actually, consciously promoted their sexuality I think it's just a hoot. Of course, they could look at me now and go, 'What!?'"

"The whole *Phedre* company was crying with laughter. I may play old boots, and I may look like a right old boot in *The American*," she joked, referring to a forgettable U.S. TV movie based on a James Joyce novel of the same name. "But who cares if I'm that sexy? It's lent a new spring to my step." When asked the secret to maintaining her lithe physique, Rigg credits moderation and activity. But while she enjoys tennis and swimming, don't expect to see her at the local gym. "I absolutely loathe the idea of standing in a classroom, doing regimental exercises," she said.

Rigg was in for another surprise a short time later when *TV Guide* went one step further and named Dame Diana the sexiest television star of all time, beating out other one-time heartthrobs such as Tom Selleck, Richard Chamberlain and Farrah Fawcett. Then-managing editor Jack Curry said: "She has the power of the British bird. Give them a British accent and some Carnaby Street clothes and Americans will love it. Sex appeal and brains is a combination that most American actresses don't have."

"Well . . . there ya go," Rigg laughed to Brett Thomas. "It's a hoot. I am deeply honored but a bit confused—I was only ever a B-cup. I never played sex. Nowadays you see a lot of actresses who are kind of peddling it, and good luck to them, but I never played it, so it always came as a surprise." Just to round out her legacy, *TV Guide* also listed Emma Peel number eight in a piece on "TV's 50 Greatest Characters Ever."

The surge of interest in Peel and Rigg not-so-coincidentally coincided with the hoopla surrounding the 1998 big-screen release of *The Avengers*, starring Ralph Fiennes and Uma Thurman. Had not Rigg and *The Avengers* TV series become such icons, the movie might have stood a chance to succeed on the merits of its kitsch story line of Steed and Peel having to save the world from a mad scientist and his weather-altering machine. But the original is so burned into the pop-culture subconscious that there was no way for the movie to live up to the expectations set by the series. Thurman bore the brunt of the critical barbs, which just confirmed how indelibly Peel and Rigg were associated by generations of all ages.

When asked by the *Sunday Times* shortly after the movie's release if she had seen it, Rigg said, "No, not yet. It opened just before I opened in the West End, so I haven't had the time. I think I'll wait till it comes out on video; I'd rather watch it alone. Besides, I'd be too embarrassed to be seen going into a showing in a cinema. 'Oh look,' they'd say, 'it's her.'" Dame Diana also denied hearing rumors producers of the film wanted to ask her to appear in a cameo. "I've no idea," she said, "but I wouldn't have done it. That would have been . . . inappropriate." While Rigg found the attention and honors an enjoyable acknowledgement of her work and legacy, it had the additional effect of deepening the shadow Rachael found herself in. She wasn't just the daughter of a successful actress or star; she was the daughter of a legend and icon. So forging an identity separate from her mother's became a near-obsession because Rachael Stirling did not want to be given roles based on her heritage; she wanted to succeed as an actress in her own right.

Rachael Stirling, taken at the 1999 Berlin Film Festival

"I was by no means pushed—if anything, held back by the scruff of the neck," Rachael said. "I got into acting because it was the only thing that fulfilled me. But I got into it by myself. I joined the National Youth Theatre undercover; no one knew who Mama was.

"It's been a blessing and a curse being the daughter

of Diana Rigg. I'm hugely proud of her and have learned a vast amount from her. But I had to find out for myself if I was any good at this, and before I could, people were making comparisons. In England, everybody's quick to pounce and say, 'You only got that job because . . .' That was fucking frustrating! I've never once gotten through a door because Mama's made a call. Well, she might have helped me get an audition, but *never* a job. And so I just took precautions and decided to go it on my own until I had done enough to be able to stand up and say, 'She's my ma, but I did it on my own.'"

But Stirling also admits, "I think I was almost too cagey about my mother. I hadn't dealt with it very well. I didn't really know how to, so I went completely undercover. I got an agent on my own and got into the National Youth Theatre on my own. I did it all on my own and that is important when you are trying to find your own way. But I am so proud of her and it took a long time for me to acknowledge that in public. I felt it would take away from what I did."

As Rachael began to be recognized for her own talents, she gave an interesting perspective on the family home, particularly on her own tumultuous teen years, when her parents' marriage was dissolving. She revealed to the *Sunday Mirror* that she chose to go to boarding school rather than stay home during that time. She explained, "I was given a choice of schools, and from the age of eleven to eighteen I went to Wycombe Abbey girls' school where I had an incredible education. It is one of the top schools in the country and they give you the confidence to believe that you can do, and be, anything. That is the privilege of private education."

The downside was the traditional hazing by older students. "They put us through tests to see what we knew," Rachael said. "We were petrified. It was all about power, so it was cruel in a sense. But at the same time, no sooner are you grown up than you can't wait to turn the tables and do the same thing to the younger ones. Boys' bullying is well-publicized, but girls' bullying is much more psychological—more malicious. It is an almighty thing to go away from home to school and be disillusioned at the age of eleven and a half. I am not sure that I would send my own children to a boarding school. I was okay because I was equipped to deal with it, but not all children are."

Despite the hazing, Stirling says the boarding school was preferable to being at home, but not because of the divorce—because of being a volatile teenager. She explained, "You go through a weird patch when you start going through puberty and it's fine because you have spent your fury and your frustration at the structure which is boarding school and its staff, who represent authority. By venting your feelings on them, instead of your parents, your parents remain important, separate and sacred."

It is more than a little ironic that Dame Diana, who happily put parenting before career and, along with Archie, successfully instilled a strong sense of ambition and independence in her child, should continue to portray such flawed mothers onstage. Rigg's most recent triumph was in the Royal National Theatre's 1991 production of *Humble Boy*, written by Charlotte Jones. Reminiscent of Tom Stoppard's style, the play is full of deep ideas presented very accessibly through touching pathos and genuine humor. The story revolves around thirty-five-year-old Felix Humble, a Cambridge astrophysicist searching for a unified field theory. Following the sudden death of his father, he returns home to be with his difficult and demanding mother, who he discovers is contemplating marriage to her lover. In this obliquely updated version of *Hamlet*, Jones explores the familial ties that bind—or, in Felix jargon, unify. The *Evening Standard* wrote: "Death, theoretical astrophysics, and bees form the heart of Charlotte Jones's latest comedy, which sparkles with eccentric humor and is as tightly structured as a honeycomb. . . . For this production, Diana Rigg plays Felix's mother Flora Humble, all hard heart, sharp heels and back-copies of *Vogue*. . . . When Flora dismisses her husband's colleagues as a 'boredom of entomologists' you can see the dashed dreams of her glamorized youth; when Felix—a theoretical astrophysicist—in turn compares her magnetism to the destructive pull of a black hole, you start to understand why he is such an apology for manhood."

Kate Kellaway of the *Observer* said, "As Felix's mother, Diana Rigg looks like a queen bee with her black sunglasses and smooth, blonde head. . . . Her appearance and her manners are in stark contrast to each other. She is groomed, politely dressed, but there is nothing coifed about her anger, her despair at her own life. It is a brilliant portrait with a performance to match."

The *Financial Times* added: "Diana Rigg as Flora gives her best—her least camply theatrical, her most interestingly self-contradictory—performance in maybe 15 years."

But for every glowing review, there was always a balancing opinion that would prevent Rigg from letting her accolades go too much to her head. In late October 2001, Dame Diana participated in a fund-raising performance of Clare Boothe Luce's play, *The Women*. In the middle of the play, as Rigg was speaking some dialogue, she was interrupted by a woman in the audience who took issue with the play's relentless wit. "What a load of fucking drivel!" the disgruntled patron yelled at the stage. "This is the worst play I have ever seen in my life. Get me out of here." Her extremely embarrassed companion dragged her out, against her will, helped by a frantic theater staff. Before being pushed out, the woman managed to thwack a few other patrons on their heads with her program, and even when finally in the lobby, she was still audible to the audience, yelling, "I forked out £125 to watch fucking drivel!" Throughout the tirade, Rigg continued on without missing a beat. Afterwards, cast member Cherie Lunghi told several reporters: "I think the story line might have touched a raw nerve. Diana Rigg did a splendid job to continue the way she did."

Fortunately, most patrons were thrilled to watch Rigg onstage. But while *Humble Boy* may have been just another successful performance to add to her resume, it may have also been a kind of theatrical swan song. In talking to John Koch of the *Boston Globe*, Dame Diana acknowledged she was slowing down and that there really were no roles she yearned to play anymore. "No! I have a relish for my work—I love it. But I don't have the hunger of the young," she said. "It's almost akin to envy in a way: *'Oh, I'd love to do that. Wouldn't it be wonderful.'* I think as you get older, that falls away from you. Well, it did to me." She also admitted her intelligence now got in the way sometimes. "There are occasions when you look at the text and think, *'This won't do'*, but you can't rewrite it," she said. On a lighter note, Rigg joked that there was *one* role that appealed to her: "I'd love to be a Bond baddie. It's about time they had a really, really bad woman—and I could do that easily."

But it was clear that Rigg had begun to prepare herself for the inevitable, both personally and professionally. "It's the nature of our profession that you get supplanted by someone else, no matter how great you are," she observed in a *Time Out* interview. "The memory of what you've done eventually gets eclipsed by the ensuing generation. That's the way it should be. Every so often I get defensive about it. Of course I see my body changing and decrepitude creeping in. But it's really part of the process of living. And if I really want to feel old, I can see myself in black and white." But she did make a case for producers not abandoning female actors as they age. "Traditionally, there will always be more big parts for men," she said. "But it's interesting. I don't want to sound contentious, but I actually think more female stars sell tickets than males."

More and more, Rigg mused on the process of getting older. Shortly after her sixtieth birthday in 1998, Dame Diana told the *Sunday Telegraph Magazine* she felt "terrific about the whole thing." She went on, "It's a gaaas. I've really got to sort out my pension and my bus pass. But how do I feel about turning sixty? Well, I love the seasons, and so the prospect of only having fifteen springs left and fifteen autumns—that is, if I have the average lifespan—gives me pause for thought. But it doesn't depress me. No point in beating your breast and crying, 'I'm old, I'm old.' I don't think I can complain too much, really."

Rigg dealt with aging by alternating between philosophical waxing to good-humored self-mocking. "You can't eat spinach anymore because of the risk of that Limpopo green smile. You can't get on top of your lover in broad daylight. And some days you wake up feeling 104 and you have to treat yourself very, very nicely," she said.

She also observed to Gyles Brandreth in 2001, "There are things like under the chin that are very obvious to you as a person, which are just awful. And then there are the droops— the bosoms, the bottom, the jowls." Despite previous denials, she finally admitted, "I had a nip about ten years ago, but I can't be bothered now. I let Coral Browne (Vincent Price's wife) be a warning. She had her face done to the extent that when she smiled it was a terrible effort to get the lips back over her teeth again." Having been in the public eye for so long, Rigg also admitted it was sort of silly to try to recapture a long-ago look, like some of her contemporaries have. "I'd feel foolish," she said. "I don't think they are, but I would, because everybody knows I'm sixty. And the *Avengers* girl I was then, I don't think would translate to a sixty-year-old."

Even if Diana was now a proud pensioner, it didn't mean she had lost her appeal. But in one particular case, she would have preferred to be a lot less desirable. Throughout her career, Diana the actress had managed her celebrity in such a way so that it hadn't interfered with Diana the person. Rigg has never traveled with an entourage. She also prefers walking city streets to absorb their sights, smells and sounds, rather than be isolated in a limo or town car, and she still goes grocery shopping for herself. This determination to experience the nuts and bolts of daily living is laudable for any public person and says a lot about his or her character and personality. But what makes it particularly telling in Rigg's case is that she did it despite being a stalker's object of obsessive desire for nearly twenty years.

During that time, an avalanche of obscene letters accompanied by pornographic photos had been sent to Rigg, and authorities had been unable to suss out the identity of the apparently crazed fan—until Rigg took the letters to the press in 1992. "I have very little anticipation that he'll be caught," she said. "I just wanted to give him the shock of his life." But as soon as the letters were printed, several other prominent actresses, including Lauren Bacall, Helen Mirren and two actresses with an *Avengers* connection—Honor Blackman and Joanna Lumley—also came forward to say that they too had been sent obscene letters by the same obsessed fan. Altogether, there were over 2,000 letters. One common thread was that all the actresses were, as the police delicately observed, "of a certain age."

Although stalkers are recognized as a legitimate potential threat, one of the actresses involved suggested British police had initially been less than aggressive in their investigation. Seventy-eight-year-old Moira Lister, the first to contact police about the stalker, told the *Independent*, "I became very frightened about leaving the stage door and was very wary of anyone loitering. Not a lot appears to have been done by the police after I first contacted them several years ago. But this time, because of the Jill Dando murder, they became interested in tracking this man down."

Dando had been a host on the series *Crimewatch*, the British version of *America's Most Wanted*. In 1999, an obsessed fan named Barry George shot and killed Dando on the front steps of her home in a crime eerily reminiscent of Rebecca Schaeffer's murder. Schaeffer, who costarred on the sitcom *My Sister Sam* opposite Pam Dawber, was shot by Robert Bardo, who had tracked down her home address through a private detective.

Once police started investigating, they uncovered the extent of the stalking. Detective Sgt. Shirley McGlone told crime correspondent John Steele, "We submitted Miss Lister's letters to the Forensic Science Service Laboratory and found that this was one episode of a long series which dates back to 1982. We believe it might go back even further, perhaps even to the late 1970s.

"Many of the ladies have received numerous letters. Some throw them away as soon as they recognize the distinctive envelopes. Others find them deeply upsetting. Obviously, these letters have a different effect on different people. I can say, however, that all of the victims want us to catch this person."

The officer stressed that there was no suggestion that the stalker was an imminent threat, "as whoever is responsible has been writing these letters for years." She added, "However, there is a psychological impact which could be described as an assault." Police were hoping that DNA collected from the envelopes and the stalker's distinctive handwriting would allow them to identify him should a suspect turn up. Ironically, it was only after the story was aired on *Crimewatch* that a tip came in that finally led police to the most unlikely celebrity stalker.

In April 2001, police apprehended seventy-two-year-old Raymond Baker, a retired civil service worker, and held him on suspicion of creating a public nuisance. Baker, a widower whom the press would dub the "Silver Stalker," denied he was a stalker. He told the *Mirror* he had never heard of some of the actresses he was accused of writing. "I can't understand why the police have spoken to me," he said. "I have no criminal record and I am of good character. I don't write many letters either, and I always print letters I do write." Interestingly, Baker had trained as an actor in the early 1960s but was forced to quit acting after he was unable to make a living at it. Despite his protestations of innocence, forensic evidence proved his guilt, thus ending one of the more disturbing chapters in Rigg's professional career.

It's more than a little ironic that a woman so desired by men of all ages over the span of five decades should find herself unattached. But rather than be bitter, Rigg chose a Zen acceptance. She explained, "When I was young, women were considered incomplete without a husband, and it has taken me years and years and years to come to the tranquil conclusion that life can be complete without a man." That said, Dame Diana wasn't shutting the door to possible romance: "I am not on the prowl—there is nothing worse than a woman on the hunt—but I am always open. The door is always open. Always."

Always proactive, Diana decided in 2002 that it was time for a change, so she bought a house in France and starting spending time there refurbishing. Although she was quoted as saying, "I have no appetite for work now. I'm too busy grappling with my plumbers and workmen in France," she has since costarred in the 2003 A&E/BBC miniseries *Charles II* as Henrietta Marie of France, her hunger to take on new roles obviously undiminished. But Rigg has always been a star performer who reveled in her time off to enjoy life. So it's in keeping with this balancing act that the same woman who will perform three plays in repertory will also at times desire to step back from it all.

"I want to press rewind," she remarked. "I want to find rural, and you can't in England, so I've found it in France, in Landes, in a village without a shop, just a handful of houses and a tenth-century church." But that didn't mean she was turning into a wallflower. "I hope there's a tinge of disgrace about me," Rigg told the *Sunday Times*. "Hopefully, there's one good scandal left in me yet—one surprising thing, yah?"

In 2003, Dame Diana was indeed involved in a scandal, but not the type she probably had in mind. In September 2002, the *Daily Mail* published an interview written by Jane Kelly. The headline read: 'Diana Rigg attacks British men and announces her retirement.' In the piece, Kelly wrote:

"English men are intimidated by me," she says, suddenly spreading her long arms wide in a gesture of resignation. "But I'm not concerned with the effect I have on men," she says defiantly.

"I don't think about it. You know I am beyond feeling disappointed." Her voice swoops down on certain words like a great bird. "I love the company of men, they are adorable (she says this as if she is talking about pugs or terriers), but I am devastated at what has happened."

She means the fate of most women in Britain, even beautiful ones like her, when they hit middle age. "I have completely disappeared," she booms. "I am totally invisible." No one finds this situation easy, least of all a woman worshipped by men. . . .

Now past the middle of her "journey," she seems resolved and optimistic. She is also probably at the height of her powers as an actress.

"I've decided to retire," she says quietly, and it is typical of her to announce something so dramatic in such a teasing, insouciant way.

When Rigg read the article, her long-simmering resentment of the "grubettes" finally boiled over. She retained an attorney and sued the paper. Her lawyer, Tom Amlot, explained the action: "Dame Diana was upset at the portrayal of her which quite wrongly suggested that she is an embittered woman and holds British men in low regard. She was also concerned that her professional reputation and ability to secure work would be damaged by the statement that she was retiring when she is not."

It should be noted that the libel laws in the U.S. and England are glaringly different. British libel laws are considered pro-plaintiff, meaning that the defendant must prove that he or she did not commit libel. This is the opposite of American libel law, which places the burden of proof upon the plaintiff to show that the alleged libelous statement contained malice and caused damage. More striking is that in America, you cannot be convicted of libel if what you write is the truth. No matter how embarrassing or in how bad of a light it puts someone, truth is the final determiner. In England, you can be sued for writing something that is one hundred percent accurate if you write it knowing it might cause harm to the individual's professional "good name."

Dame Diana told her side of the story to London's *Daily Telegraph*: "I don't generally give interviews unless I have to promote a play and had sworn years ago, having been bitten once too often, never to be interviewed by a woman again. Of course, not all female journalists are bad, but many in our tabloid papers lead the world in exercising malice. But this interview was different; it was for a charity, Children With AIDS, and I had been approached by its fund director, Peter Brooke Turner, to raise awareness of its needs."

Rigg says she agreed to meet with Kelly to talk specifically about the charity and had Turner accompany her. "The interview, I remember, proceeded rather jerkily as she kept pulling away from the subject of the charity into more personal matters and I kept pulling her back," Diana recalls. "In the end I gave in and responded in general terms to questions on childhood, early theater, the new house in France, etcetera. Nothing I hadn't spoken about before, and we seemed to part on cordial terms."

But two days later when the article appeared, Dame Diana said she went into shock: "I had been given a persona I didn't recognize, attitudes I don't possess, opinions I don't hold and words I had not spoken. To cap it all, Miss Kelly had decided to retire me." Rigg's friends all advised her to shrug it off because few people would remember the article the next day. But Dame Diana decided to take a stand against the paper, worried the picture painted of her would be reprinted elsewhere. She retained the services of Harbottle and Lewis attorney Tom Amlot. "He looked young enough to be my grandson, with spiky hair and a huge gap-toothed grin," she said. Although Amlot was convinced Rigg stood a good chance of winning, he warned her victory would have a heavy price tag. "Tom handed me a list of charges and warned me telephone calls would be timed," she recalled. "I renamed him 'Start-the-Clock' Amlot."

At that point, it became a war of attorneys, with the paper vigorously defending the story and backing the journalist. Whether it was a display of solidarity or an unwise knee-jerk reaction, the *Daily Mail* subsequently published a picture taken of Rigg in France along with another Jane Kelly article titled 'Looking for love in France'. Rigg's blood pressure spiked. "I had been followed to a remote village and secretly photographed," she explained. "The article claimed I was living 'the life of a recluse' in France and was accompanied by a grim photograph of me clutching a baguette. The caption read, 'Shopping for one.' Much of the original article was reprinted. Why print this? Was it there to substantiate the retirement claim? Or possibly to intimidate me, leaving me in no doubt that there wasn't a corner of my life the *Mail* could not expose? I will never know, but people still stop me in the street and ask why I am here and not in France. Irritating."

One point in Rigg's favor was having Turner as an eyewitness to back up her account of what was and wasn't said during the interview. But the legal wrangling dragged on. "Gradually the tactics became clear," Rigg told the *Telegraph*. "The opposition intended to drag the proceedings out as long as possible, incurring hair-raising legal bills, in the hope that I would run out of steam or money or both. 'Start-the-Clock' kept my spirits up and urged me to hang on in there, but it wasn't easy."

Eventually, the tabloid offered to make an apology and a settlement was reached. Rigg was awarded $48,000 at London's High Court for libel and invasion of privacy. The *Evening Standard* and *Daily Mail* newspapers, which published the articles, were also ordered to pay her legal fees of $134,000. "Am I happy at the outcome?" Rigg asked rhetorically. "Of course, but the past months have held moments of deep depression. Archie, my ex, must have been hugely embarrassed by the article but never for a moment taxed me for it. My brother and his family had read the bit about 'her father was strange' but rallied to my side. It tends to be overlooked that many people are indirectly affected by thoughtless and cruel journalism.

"What now? Top of my agenda is a celebratory lunch at The Ivy with 'Start-the-Clock,' which promises to be fun. I am paying, natch."

While Diana was immersed in her lawsuit, Rachael Stirling was stirring up some media interest of her own as the star of the BBC miniseries *Tipping the Velvet*, Andrew Davies' adaptation of Sarah Waters' novel about the lesbian underworld of Victorian England. Billed by network publicists as the "steamiest show ever seen on TV," Stirling stars as Nan, who goes on a long journey of self-discovery after falling in love with a bisexual named Kitty.

When asked by Brett Thomas about her daughter's role in the movie, Rigg answered with delight, "She's playing a les-

• • • •

bian. She went and had lesbian lessons. God knows why. She was sent by the BBC, along with the girl with whom she has this lesbian love scene. Lesbian lessons! Is that not extraordinary? Ha!" But Rigg's pride was obvious: "My daughter is the most important person in my life. She has my work ethic and her father's relish for life."

Stirling reported that her mother "blubbed"—the English word for cried—"all the way through with pride." She added affectionately, "It was pathetic." While she felt at ease with her mom watching the love scenes, it was a little more uncomfortable with her father. "I had to scream, 'Eyes on sandals!' at him when we were watching a scene with breasts everywhere. That's what he used to say to me when I was watching a snogging scene on, say, *Dynasty*, which he didn't think was suitable," she said.

The movie's graphic love scenes between Rachael and costar Keely Hawes, which included a close encounter with a giant golden dildo, had the British tabloid tongues wagging. Like her mother had been forced to do years earlier, Stirling defended the nudity and the content and dismissed the prurient interest as misplaced. She explained, "The point about the sex, actually, was that it had to be completely realistic, otherwise there was not a point, and it had to be passionate. It was Nan's first love affair—she goes to the theater and she sees this creature, Kitty, onstage and falls in love instantly. And it was that naïve trepidation at being able to touch the one you love for the first time, combined with absolute passion, so the two of us, we went for it hammer and tongs. There was no point in doing anything else, really."

Stirling admits that a couple of cocktails helped loosen her inhibitions: "Before I did that gold, naked dildo scene, I tell you what, I'm from Scotland, I had a dram or two behind the scenes. Everybody else in the room was clothed, and I had to wear this leather enormous strap-on. It's about that big! It weighs a ton!

"Keely and I, who'd worked together on *Othello* and previously on something else, used to sit in the dressing room and have a couple of glasses of dry white wine and say, 'Here's to it.' And then off we went onto set and snogged happily," Rachael said.

During a press conference, Stirling's costar John Bowe, who plays the man Kitty eventually marries, remembered: "Geoff Sax, the director, after we'd all first met for the first read-through, said, 'I'd like to point out that clearly there are some very dangerous and explicit love scenes on this show, and on the days that we shoot those scenes, I will be reducing the number of crew on the set, and only the camera operator, the director of photography, the focus puller, myself—and the winner of the daily lottery will be allowed to go on the set.' That kind of broke the ice. But anyone who's done sex scenes—naked sex scenes—as I have, and now Rachael, on television, knows that they are the most mechanical, asexual experience of your life."

Displaying a bit of her inherited innate sense of timing, Rachael looked at Bowe, paused and then quipped, "Maybe that's 'cause *you're* not doing 'em right, babe." Her mother's daughter indeed.

When she was thirty-seven, writer Lawrence B. Eisenberg had asked Rigg what she foresaw for herself in thirty years. She immediately quipped, "A dirty old woman," then became thoughtful. "When I'm sixty-six, I hope I'm . . . alive, I'm in one piece, that I am independent, physically and financially, that I've learned a great deal more than I have up until this stage and that I'm a raver of a sixty-seven-year-old, you know, fun to be with and joyous, laughing a great deal and, hopefully, a couple of lovers." By and large, she has met her own expectations.

Dame Diana Rigg likes to speak of her life as her "journey," and now with more traveled road behind her than in front, she embraces ever more closely the things that bring joy. "I believe in laughter," she says. "I think it's the greatest catalyst of all time. It's wonderful. It explodes pomposity, sadness, inhibitions. Anytime is a perfect time to joke." Which explains why the woman who will go down as one of the great dramatic actors of all time wants her epitaph to read: "If the earth moves, she's laughing."

DIANA RIGG'S NOTABLE PERFORMANCES AND AWARDS

Film and Television

2003: *Charles II* (miniseries)—Henrietta Marie of France

2002: *Broadway: The Golden Age, by the Legends Who Were There*—Herself

2002: *Cannon Movie Tales: Cinderella*—Lady Maude Triklay

2001: *Victoria and Albert* (miniseries)—Baroness Lehzen

2000: *In the Beginning* (miniseries)—Rebeccah

1998–2000: *The Mrs. Bradley Mysteries* (TV series)—Mrs. Adela Bradley

1998: *The American* (TV)—Madame de Bellegarde

1998: *Parting Shots*—Lisa

1997: *Rebecca* (TV)—Mrs. Danvers

1996: *Samson and Delilah* (TV)—Mara

1996: *The Fortunes and Misfortunes of Moll Flanders* (TV)—Mrs. Golightly

1995: *The Haunting of Helen Walker* (TV)—Mrs. Grose

1995: *Danielle Steel's Zoya* (TV)—Countess Evgenia

1994: *Running Delilah* (TV)—Judith

1994: *A Good Man in Africa*—Chloe Fanshawe

1993: *Genghis Cohn*—Baroness Frieda von Stangel

1992: *Mrs. 'Arris goes to Paris* (TV)—Madame Colbert

1989–1998: *Mystery!* (TV series)—Hostess

1989: *Unexplained Laughter* (TV)—Lydia

1989: *Mother Love* (miniseries)—Helena Vesey

1987: *A Hazard of Hearts* (TV)—Lady Harriet Vulcan

1987: *Snow White*—Evil Queen

1986: *The Worst Witch* (TV)—Miss Hardbroom

1985: *Bleak House* (miniseries)—Lady Dedlock

1984: *King Lear* (TV)—Regan

1982: *Evil Under the Sun*—Arlena Marshall

1982: *Little Eyolf* (TV)—Rita Allmers

1982: *Witness for the Prosecution* (TV)—Christine Vole

1981: *The Great Muppet Caper*—Lady Holiday

1980: *The Marquise* (TV)—Eloise La Marquise d'Casternell

1979: *The Serpent Son* (miniseries)—Kytamnestra

1977: *A Little Night Music*—Charlotte Mittelheim

1977: *Three Piece Suite* (TV)—various

1975: *In This House of Brede* (TV)—Philippa Talbot (Emmy nomination)

1973: *Diana* (TV series)—Diana Smythe

1973: *Theatre of Blood*—Edwina Lionheart

1971: *The Hospital*—Barbara Drummond

1970: *Julius Caesar* (TV)—Portia

1970: *Married Alive* (TV)—Liz Jardine

1969: *On Her Majesty's Secret Service*—Tracy / Contessa Theresa

1969: *The Assassination Bureau*—Miss Winters

1968: *A Midsummer Night's Dream*—Helena

1965–1967: *The Avengers* (TV series)—Emma Peel (Emmy nomination)

1965: *Blood and Thunder*, "Women Beware Women" episode (TV)

1964: *The Comedy of Errors* (TV)—Adriana

1964: *The Hothouse* (TV)—Anita Fender

TV GUEST APPEARANCES

2001: *Wish You Were Here . . . ?*, "Visits Scotland 2001" episode—Herself

1993: *Road to Avonlea*, "The Disappearance" episode—Lady Blackwell

1969: *The Morecambe and Wise Show*—Herself

1963: *The Sentimental Agent*, "A Very Desirable Plot" episode—Francy

THEATER

(London productions, unless otherwise noted)

2001: *Humble Boy*—Flora

1999: *Britannicus/Phedre*—Phedre

1996–1997: *Who's Afraid of Virginia Woolf?*—Martha (New York)

1995–1996: *Mother Courage and Her Children*—Anna Fierling

1994: *Medea*—Medea (New York; Olivier Award nomination)

1993: *Medea*—Medea

1990: *All for Love*—Cleopatra

1987: *Follies*—Phyllis

1982: *Colette*—Colette

1978–1979: *Night and Day*—Ruth Carson

1975: *Phaedra Brittanica*—The Governor's Wife

1974: *The Misanthrope*—Célimène (Tony nomination)

1974: *Pygmalion*—Eliza Doolittle

1972: *Macbeth*—Lady Macbeth

1971: *Abelard and Heloise*—Heloise (New York; Tony nomination)

1970: *Abelard and Heloise*—Heloise

1970: *Jumpers*—Dolly

1966: *Twelfth Night*—Viola (RSC in Stratford)

1963: *King Lear*—Cordelia (RSC in Stratford)

1961: *A Midsummer Night's Dream*—Helena (RSC in Stratford)

1961: *The Devils*—Philippe Trincant

1960: *Troilus and Cressida*—Andromache (RSC in Stratford)

1957: *The Caucasian Chalk Circle*—Natella Abashwili (York Festival)

AWARDS

1997: Emmy Award for *Rebecca*

1996: Evening Standard Award for *Who's Afraid of Virginia Woolf?*

1995: Evening Standard Award for *Mother Courage and Her Children*

1994: Tony Award for *Medea*

1993: Evening Standard Award for *Medea*

1982: Variety Club Award for *Evil Under the Sun*

1970: Critics Award for *Abelard and Heloise*